E
GE
OF
HELLENISM

DE
77
.F37
1973

THE HERITAGE OF HELLENISM

THE GREEK WORLD
FROM 323 BC TO 31 BC

JOHN FERGUSON

with 77 illustrations, 9 in color

HARCOURT BRACE JOVANOVICH, INC.

For U.M.

First American edition 1973

ISBN 0-15-535723-9

Library of Congress Catalog Card Number: 72-81187

Printed in Great Britain by Jarrold and Sons Ltd, Norwich

CONTENTS

FOREWORD

This book does not require an elaborate prologue. It is an attempt to draw a sketch of the Hellenistic age, of the culture, that is, of the eastern Mediterranean from Alexander's death in 323 BC to the establishment of Augustus' authority at Actium in 31 BC, with some spillover. It is not a history in the conventional sense: though I owe to Martin Charlesworth most of what I know of the classical world, I am not a historian *pur sang*. It is an impression, or series of impressions, of different aspects of the age. In accordance with the policy of the editor of the Library of European Civilization, Professor Geoffrey Barraclough, I have tried to pay special attention to the continuity of tradition: the Hellenistic age is an age which, it is easy to see, springs from the past and points to the future.

I have incorporated some material from my paper 'The Children of Heaven and the Children of the Sun', given on a number of occasions, and published in *Nigeria and the Classics*, 1964. Versions of Callimachus come from my article 'The Epigrams of Callimachus', in *Greece and Rome*, 1970. All translations, unless otherwise attributed, are my own.

I owe a number of debts of gratitude: to Professor Barraclough, for inviting me to undertake a labour of love; to the staff of Thames and Hudson, for their skilled and sympathetic approach to book production, for advice on specific points, and especially for their pursuit of the illustrative material on which this series so justly depends; to my colleague, Gary Rees, for his co-operative clarity in the provision of maps; to my wife Elnora for undertaking yet another index; to my friend and secretary, Lesley Roff, for the exactingly high standards of her patient and cheerful diligence.

J. F.

I COSMOPOLIS

In 334 BC Alexander crossed the Hellespont from Europe to Asia, and the world was never the same again. He swept through Asia Minor – past Syria to Egypt – down through Mesopotamia – up by Hamadan and the Caspian Gates, through the Hindu Kush to Samarkand and the neighbourhood of Tashkent – down into Kashmir and across the Indus to the Beas, where the troops mutinied. It was incredible, breath-taking. At one point he and his army covered four hundred miles in ten days. He had dreamed of reaching Ocean, the great river which in Greek thought encircled the land-mass of the world, of giving his Greeks an outlet to the sea which they felt to be their home, of solving the ravelled problems of the geographers. But his troops would go no further. For a time he sulked like his hero Achilles, then he turned back down to Karachi, north-westwards along the coast, and so amid bitter privation inland back to Susa.

He left Greece with Aristotle and Isocrates as the background of his thinking. Aristotle had taught him that Greeks and Greeks alone had full and true humanity; foreigners, *barbaroi* (people who make unintelligible noises such as *bar-bar* instead of speaking a pellucid tongue like Greek), were by nature slaves, and a slave was a tool endowed with life. Isocrates had yearned for Greek unity, and seen that in the sin of this world (though he would not so have put it) unity is most easily attained in opposition to a common enemy. America and Russia found unity against the Nazis, and would find unity again if the world were threatened with invasion from Mars. Isocrates hoped to find Greek unity in renewing the old crusade against Persia, and, when the Greek states took no initiative, looked to an individual, Nicocles or Dionysius, Philip or Alexander, to lead that crusade. Alexander, crusading against the barbarians with Homer under his pillow, came to find Greeks who let him down, and Asiatics whom he could respect as opponents, like Memnon, or trust as administrators, like Ada. Practical experience led to the rejection of Aristotle and Isocrates, and a policy of fusion. He and eighty of his officers ceremoniously married Persian girls; ten thousand of his troops married their Asiatic concubines. Alexander made ready to admit Persian troops to his army, but the army showed signs of discontent. Alexander dismissed them and prepared to form an army of Persians. The Macedonians protested, 'You have made the Persians your kinsmen'; he answered, 'But I make you all my kinsmen', and, in a scene of cheering and weeping, reconciliation was won. At a celebrated banquet, of which much has been made, Alexander prayed for concord and partnership in empire between Greeks and Persians.

Was there more to it than that? Sir William Tarn thought that there was. Alexander, he claimed, had a vision, for the first time in history, of the unity of mankind. This view has been radically and persuasively criticized by Dr Badian and others, though one cannot help feeling that if the old lion were still with us he would raise a by no means impotent claw against his adversaries. Four passages in our sources have been claimed in support of Tarn's view. First, while Alexander was in Egypt we are told that he visited the oracle of Zeus-Ammon in the desert, and received the revelation that he was the god's son. Enough has not been made of the fact that this was Siwa, not Delphi or Dodona, and the god who gave the oracle was not pan-Hellenic but international in a wider sense. Shortly after this we are told that he was pleased with the saying, 'God is the king of all men' (a Homeric commonplace), but went further and reached the wise conclusion that God is the common father of all mankind but makes the best men peculiarly his own. In its context in Egypt this suggests that God judges by inner quality and not by race.

Secondly, the banquet at Opis was imaginatively reconstructed by Tarn; this reconstruction has been roughly handled by Badian in particular, and probably nothing now can be built on it, though, without accepting Tarn's mistranslation of Alexander's words, I wonder whether they were not deliberately ambiguous. It would be a little odd for a man who, as Badian says, 'did not gain his empire by well-meaning muddleheadedness' to administer a pointed snub to those present from within the empire who were neither Greek nor Persian. Still, the idea that this was an international love-feast must probably be abandoned.

Thirdly, a passage in Plutarch specifically says that Alexander believed himself to have a mission from God to harmonize men generally, and to be the reconciler of the world (an astonishing phrase),

8

1 A fanciful depiction of the birth of Alexander in a mosaic from Baalbek

bringing men from everywhere into a unity and mixing their lives and customs, their marriages and social ways, as in a loving-cup. This *may* be early Empire rhetoric; if so it is very striking, and there is no particular reason to suppose that Plutarch did not find it in one of his sources, even if that were not, as Tarn claimed, Eratosthenes.

Fourthly, there is a passage from Eratosthenes, a good source, stating specifically that Alexander ignored the advice to treat Greeks as friends and non-Greeks as enemies, and received and favoured *all men* of good repute.

There is enough here to suggest that Alexander's thinking had reached beyond the policy of fusion, even if he had not gone as far as

Tarn claimed. Certainly he is a turning point. Behind him lay the squabbles of city-states and conflicts of nations. In front of him lay Stoics and Epicureans who in a newly broken world proclaimed the unity of mankind against the realities of their day. It is not long before we find Eratosthenes blaming those who, like Aristotle and unlike Alexander, divided men into Greek and barbarian, friend and enemy, and calling instead for a moral division in which bad Greeks would be found with bad men everywhere, and good Greeks with other highly educated people, such as Indians and Persians, or politically skilled people, such as Carthaginians and Romans.

Do you say that the time was ripe, and Alexander was only the instrument of that time? In a sense you will be right. The psychological moment, which some call the fullness of time, is a reality. Already in the fifth century increased mastery of travel led to that knowledge of other lands which Herodotus so entertainingly retails to us. Increased leisure led to the demand for education which in its turn led to those extramural lecturers whom we call the 'sophists', breaking down the barriers as they moved from place to place. The social order led to individualism; individualism led to the study of man; the study of man led students to distinguish between practices and beliefs which lay rooted in nature and those prejudices which were artificial and conventional. And at the end of the century twenty-five years of war led to the creation of a professional class of mercenary soldiers, regardless of nationality, who again helped to break down the barriers. Yet all this had been true for nearly a century, and there is no trace of supranationalism in Isocrates, Plato or Aristotle, still less in the narrow, self-seeking, pettifogging ambitions of Demosthenes. Alexander conquered, and he, or those who came after him, drew the lessons from his conquest.

Alexander died young, desperately young. There were no plans for succession. A mentally defective half-brother and a posthumous son both succumbed to the ambitions of others. Alexander's dominant personality is nowhere more clearly seen than in the way in which men who had been pawns at his side became monarchs in their own right. No single man could hold his empire together. Perhaps he could not have done so himself. There was no single successor, no single regent. But the horizons had receded. The ambitious were no longer content with small domains. Out of the jockeyings for power new kingdoms emerged.

2 Alexander the Great.
Marble head from
Pergamum, *c.* 160 BC

In Egypt a shrewd officer named Ptolemy (later known as 'Soter'
or 'Saviour') established a new dynasty. He was perhaps the first to
discern the possibilities of a new order. He did not try to do too much.
He secured Egypt with its vast resources, and Cyrene, and Phoenicia
with its fleet. He got hold of Alexander's body, which secured his
prestige. His proclamation as king in 305 was the overt acknowledg-
ment that Alexander's domains had been divided. His brilliant
administrative powers ensured a solid economic foundation. This
work was carried on by his successor, another who preferred economic
to military expansiveness, Ptolemy Philadelphus. Their joint achievement was such that the dynasty survived through occasional crises
until the advent of Rome.

Towards the end the rulers were puppets. The last, and in some ways
the greatest, of the Ptolemies was Cleopatra VII. She discerned the
signs of the times, and saw that the future of the Mediterranean world
lay with Rome. Her ambitions were greater than those of the dynasty's
founder, as we shall see; she wanted world dominion, and to be queen
of the world she had to be queen of Rome. She came to Rome to win
it through Caesar, but Caesar was murdered. So she came to Tarsus
to win it through Antony.

> The barge she sat in, like a burnish'd throne,
> Burn'd on the water; the poop was beaten gold;
> Purple the sails, and so perfumed that

3–6 (*Left to right*) Ptolemy I (Soter), who proclaimed himself king of Egypt in 304. Demetrius I (Poliorcetes) of Macedon, an impetuous conqueror who failed to re-establish a Macedonian empire in Asia. Cleopatra Thea, daughter of Ptolemy IV, wife of three Seleucid monarchs and herself queen of Syria for twenty-nine years, five of them in conjunction with her pleasure-loving son Antiochus VIII ('Grypus'), who also appears here. Menander of Bactria, who ruled over a large area of India from *c.* 150 to 145 BC. Like Cleopatra VII he acquired a legend, and he appears in the *Milindapañha* as a great Buddhist monarch

> The winds were love-sick with them; the oars were silver;
> Which to the time of flutes kept stroke, and made
> The water, which they beat, to follow faster,
> As amorous of their strokes. For her own person
> It beggar'd all description.

But Antony was not of the stuff of which emperors are made. She made a final essay of the cold implacable Octavian. When that failed she took her life. Even the Roman poet paid his tribute. She was *non humilis mulier* (Horace); she died a queen.

Macedon had a more chequered history. Alexander had left Antipater in charge, a man of immense ability and loyalty, but of an older generation. He held the kingdom together till his death in 319. But then Macedon became for a period the plaything of fortune, and passed from hand to hand. Polyperchon was an inadequate successor. Antipater's son Cassander, Alexander's ferocious mother Olympias, a governor of Thrace named Lysimachus who for a short while exercised a far-flung dominion, Pyrrhus the ruler of Epirus and others flit briefly across the stage. The dynasty was eventually settled on the family of Antigonus, ex-governor of Central Phrygia. He was a man of vision and energy, a fine commander of troops, with some of Alexander's qualities. He swiftly secured Asia Minor. For the next twenty years the military and political history of the eastern Mediter-

ranean is dominated by his attempts to secure the sole succession. He finally succumbed to a coalition of his rivals at the battle of Ipsus in 301. His son Demetrius, who had married Antipater's daughter, had a base in Greece. From there he secured Macedon. But his generalship and personal charm were dissipated by his licentiousness and administrative indifference, and it was his son, Antigonus Gonatas, who re-established the Macedonian monarchy and its control of Greece. This was an unsophisticated monarchy with none of the complexities of Egypt, but effective in its own way. Rome came earlier here. Philip V, able but headstrong, challenged Roman intervention; his successor Perseus saw his forces annihilated at Pydna in 168.

Alexander's Asiatic empire fell to Seleucus. His emergence to power is a curiosity of history. He was not one of Alexander's great generals, and indeed was never an outstanding military leader. But some quality in him impressed Alexander, and on the king's death he was put in charge of Babylonia. From there, not without murder and adventure, he became acknowledged ruler of Syria, Mesopotamia and Iran, and secured Asia Minor. This was important: it meant that the state became Hellenized where it might have been Oriental, though Seleucus and his successors followed the principle of indirect rule, thereby ensuring that they were able to hold some of the eastern areas longer than they would have done by direct imposition. It also contributed, as we shall see, to the survival of the polis within cosmopolis. Seleucus was an outstanding administrator; Pausanias recorded that among Alexander's successors he was the one with the highest reputation for integrity. It is a memorable fact that, unlike some of his colleagues, he did not repudiate his Persian wife. In Antioch-on-the-Orontes Seleucus founded a capital city second only to Alexandria in the Hellenistic world, and from it successive monarchs named Seleucus, Antiochus or Demetrius exercised their power.

13

7 Attalus III (Philometor Euergetes), the otherwise insignificant ruler of Pergamum who in 133 B C bequeathed his kingdom to Rome, thus ending 160 years of Pergamene independence

Antioch and Alexandria were new cosmopolitan centres; Pella remained northern and provincial. Pergamum was a Greek city within the Seleucid domains. In 262 its ruler, Eumenes, was persuaded by Ptolemy II to secede. He maintained a cautious independence against a background of quarrelling dynasts. His successor Attalus took advantage of a period of Seleucid weakness to extend his power over Asia Minor; he did this by military victory over the Galatians of the interior, so establishing himself as the champion of Hellenism against 'barbarism'. Pergamum became an academic and cultural centre. Public enterprise in government textile factories and (probably) the parchment industry combined with studious taxation to develop financial prosperity. The rulers lived simply; they showed their magnificence in public works. Then Pergamene independence vanished as unexpectedly as it had begun. In 133 Attalus III bequeathed his kingdom to Rome.

Bactria formed a virtually independent kingdom: it was too remote for the Seleucids to exercise effective control. Antiochus III tried to reassert his authority in a mighty siege of Balkh, but was persuaded to withdraw, and gave one of his daughters to the king's son in marriage. This son, Demetrius I, became a great conquerer and extended the boundaries of his kingdom. The traditions are thereafter somewhat blurred. It was probably not he, but Demetrius II who established his power in the Punjab and was known to Chaucer as 'the grete Emetreus, the King of Ynde'. Hindu traditions of the period record 'Yavanes, ferocious in battle'. One of his successors, Menander, was converted to Buddhism; he appears in Buddhist tradition as Milinda. Thereafter we know little; the Punjab kingdom presumably became Indianized. Bactria eventually succumbed to the pressure of the Central Asiatic nomads. But it was a remarkable interlude.

Meanwhile the setting sun of Greek independence was casting a long shadow from Italy. In 217 Philip V of Macedon met with the Achaeans and Aetolians at Naupactus to conclude a peace treaty. Agelaus of Naupactus made the introductory speech and warned the delegates against civil war. In Italy a conflict was beginning between Carthage and Rome; whichever won was likely to endanger Greece. Agelaus was right. The Romans had already used their forces to put down piracy in the Adriatic; they had already a treaty of friendship with Egypt. But Philip V did not heed the warning. He challenged Rome.

For the moment the Roman fleet and an alliance with Pergamum held him in check. But in 203 Egypt was weak, with an infant king, and Macedon and Syria took the opportunity to attack. Egypt invoked the treaty. By 200 Rome had come in, and in 197 Flamininus defeated Philip at Cynoscephalae, forcing him to withdraw from Greece. Rome had too many internal problems to occupy Greece; Flamininus declared Greek independence and retired. But Antiochus of Syria, with Hannibal at his elbow, now began a policy of expansion. Rome was reluctant to intervene, but when his armies landed in Greece her hand was forced. In 191 the Romans drove him out of Europe, and in 190 Scipio's brother Lucius smashed him at Magnesia. His massed unwieldy troops could not stand up to the new-found mobility of the Roman legions, and his losses were 50,000 against the Romans' 400. The victors received a huge indemnity of 15,000 talents, their allies were rewarded with most of Antiochus' possessions – and the Romans again proclaimed the independence of Greece, and again withdrew.

In 179, after a reign of forty-two years, Philip died. His son Perseus continued to intrigue. The years from 172 to 168 were marked by unrest. Rome was again compelled to fight and, after three years of bungling, the manœuvrability of the legion again routed the rigidity

15

of the phalanx at Pydna in 168. Still Rome did not annex. She divided Macedon into four regions. The result was chaos, however, and in 146 a province was established and the Via Egnatia built to secure Roman military communications. At the same time there was unrest in Greece. Roman troops sacked Corinth, and a Roman city arose on the ruins. Greece was nominally independent, actually subject to the governor of Macedon. At the same time also Roman troops destroyed Carthage and established a new province in Africa.

If Rome was a dragon, she was at least a reluctant dragon. In the fifty years from 197 to 146 she annexed no new territory. The provinces of Africa and Macedon were followed by the acquisition of Asia (i.e. Asia Minor) by will from Pergamum in 133. Rome's reluctance to expand was due to the reluctance of the senatorial aristocracy to extend the numbers holding high office. But this changed, as a result of a device by which a magistrate held his power for a second year *pro consule* or *pro praetore*, exercising it in the provinces. This meant that all six praetors could be retained at Rome, and eight provincial governors were available without letting in new blood. The final takeover of the East was the work of Pompey the Great in 63; Egypt had to wait a generation longer. But Rome in taking over the Greek cosmopolis was herself taken over. Once captured, Greece took her barbarous captor captive, and brought civilization to backward Latium (Horace). The Orontes flooded the Tiber (Juvenal).

Alexander's empire covered something like 2,000,000 square miles. Contrast Attica with its puny thousand; even the Achaean League extended to no more than 8,000 square miles; Egypt had 60,000 with great tracts of desert as well; Pergamum suddenly exploded from polis into cosmopolis, and by the second century controlled 70,000 square miles. The Seleucids had the widest territory: at one time they commanded two-thirds of Alexander's empire, and even when compelled to drastic withdrawal they still had appreciably wider territory than any other dynasty. In the third century Carthage and Rome were, so to speak, in the same league, each controlling an area of from 50,000 to 70,000 square miles.

What was true of area was correspondingly true of population. The Seleucid dominion extended to some 30,000,000. Egypt was known to be the most densely populated land; Josephus tells us ancient authorities put the population at something over 8,000,000, and the most conservative estimate would hardly put it at less than 6,000,000. The total population of Attica in the age of Pericles, men, women and children, slaves and free, indigenes and immigrants, cannot have exceeded 300,000.

A general view of the age shows vast areas, vast aggregations of people and all linked by the common Hellenism of the ruling class. Trade routes opening up, to India, even to China, to Russia, even to the Baltic, to Africa even south of the Sahara, to Western Europe and the gates of the Atlantic. Movements of people, voluntary or enforced, on a new scale. Travel open as it had never been open save to a few enterprising individuals. It was left to Rome to clear the seas of pirates and the land of brigands. 'Thanks to the Romans', said Irenaeus, a late second-century bishop of Lyons, 'even we Christians can walk without fear on the roads and can travel wherever we please.' The Hellenistic rulers opened the door.

Judaism offers a particularly interesting example of the effect of cosmopolis, because of the very attachment to the Palestinian homeland and the Temple site. The deportations of the sixth century BC prepared the way. There were prisoners in Babylonia, exiles in Egypt. As the century wheeled on they spread more widely. Deutero-Isaiah called them from north and south, east and west, the very ends of the earth. Babylon collapsed before Persia in 538, and the Persian empire was broad and far. Not so many Jews returned to the homeland: some 50,000, including 7,000 slaves, under Zerubbabel, a mere 5,000 under Ezra. The rest spread, sometimes freely (and Darius II in 419 BC decreed that all Jews throughout his empire should keep the Feast of Unleavened Bread), sometimes unwillingly (as when Artaxerxes III deported numbers of Jews to the Caspian). Already, then, at the dawn of the Hellenistic age, Jewish communities extended far into Asia and Africa.

With the Hellenistic age the process continued and expanded. From the period of the Maccabees in the second century BC the centre prospered, but the Dispersion or Diaspora remained vast. We are badly informed about Mesopotamia and the East. Josephus' description of 'countless myriads whose number cannot be ascertained' may be exaggerated, but it can hardly be groundless, and we know that in the first century two Jewish brothers, Asinaeus and Anilaeus, were influential in the area around Nehardea, while in Adiabene the royal house was proselytized. Egypt certainly had vast numbers. According to *The Letter of Aristeas* Ptolemy I brought 100,000 from Palestine; the number is unreliable, not the underlying fact. Philo depicts the communities as extending 'to the boundaries of Ethiopia', and says that there were 1,000,000 Jews in Alexandria alone; the papyri and other records confirm the general picture. Syria was naturally a major area for the Dispersion: according to Josephus 18,000 were massacred in Damascus alone during the war of AD 66–70. A fourth area was Asia Minor; Antiochus actually transferred 2,000 families from Mesopotamia to Phrygia and Lydia. We have only to reflect on Paul's experience to realize the permeation of Asia Minor by Jews.

These were the principal areas only. We also know of Jews in the Crimea. Armenia encouraged Jewish immigration and some of the Armenian nobility were proud to claim Jewish ancestry. There were Jews in Arabia and Abyssinia, in Carthage and Mauretania, in Spain (as we may deduce from Paul's insistent desire to reach there) and Italy (where Vergil adapts for his fourth eclogue ideas from the Book of Isaiah in compliment to Pollio's Jewish connections, and Juvenal satirizes Jewish customs), in Greece (with particular ties with Sparta) and the islands. Jerusalem, said Herod Agrippa to Caligula, 'is the capital city, not of a single country, but of most, because of its colonies in Egypt, Phoenicia, Syria, Coele-Syria, Pamphylia, Cilicia, most of Asia Minor as far as Bithynia and the distant parts of Pontus' (Philo); he goes on to list Greek cities and islands with a substantial Jewish population. We remember the scene at Pentecost: 'Parthians, Medes, Elamites; inhabitants of Mesopotamia, of Judaea and Cappadocia, of Pontus and Asia, of Phrygia and Pamphylia, of Egypt and the districts of Libya around Cyrene; visitors from Rome, both Jews and proselytes, Cretans and Arabs, we hear them telling in their own tongues the great things God has done.' So Strabo: 'It is not easy to find any place in the habitable world that has not yet received this nation and in which it has not made its power felt.'

Two aspects of this Jewish Diaspora deserve special mention. The first is that Hellenistic Judaism is Hellenized Judaism; Hecataeus of Miletus was already commenting on this at the outset of the period. The Septuagint is witness to it; so is the later permission to recite the *Shema* in Greek or to write a bill of divorce in Greek. Greek thought permeates Ecclesiastes and the Wisdom of Solomon; even the Book of Job. The Maccabean revolt was not in origin a revolt against Greek culture but against idolatry. The Hasmonaean ruler Jonathan

◀ 8 Philo Judaeus (*c.* 30 BC–AD 45), as depicted in a medieval MS. A typical Hellenistic figure, he lived in Alexandria all his life and devoted himself to the synthesizing of Greek and Jewish tradition

9 The synagogue on Delos, testimony to the cosmopolitan population of Apollo's sacred island during the Hellenistic age, when it flourished as a banking centre and the major corn market of the Aegean

actually called the Spartans his brothers, and the tradition lasted two centuries. Philo stands before us as a thinker who holds firmly to Jewish traditions but is prepared to see them and express them in the light of Greek thought.

Secondly, cosmopolis encouraged Jewish universalism. The process can be seen during the Exile in Deutero-Isaiah. It continued into the Hellenistic age. Hence the proselytism, not least among women, who had not to leap the hurdle of circumcision; Josephus says that the Damascus persecutors distrusted their own wives. Proselytism was a controversial matter on both sides. But we have the universalist view expressed by Hillel: 'Be of the disciples of Aaron; one that loves peace and pursues peace, that loves mankind and brings them close to the Torah', and later by R. Eleazer ben Pedat: 'The Holy One, blessed be He, sent Israel into Exile among the nations only for the purpose of acquiring converts.' Philo, while not underplaying the concept of a 19 chosen people, is naturally a universalist: 'God is, and is from eternity; He that truly is is One; He has made the world and made it one world, unique as He himself is unique; and He continually exercises forethought for His creation.'

A second example of the effect of cosmopolis may be drawn from the inscriptions of Delos. The evidence of economic life is well preserved in the temple records, and shows that the Delians' interests spread all over the Aegean, to Hermione in the Argolid, for example, or Peparethus off the coast of Thessaly. More interesting, however, is the provenance of the merchants found at Delos. There are Greeks from all over the Mediterranean world, Alexandrians of course, Syrians and Phoenicians and Nabataean Arabs, traders from Yemen and the Persian Gulf, and in the later part of the period Romans and Italians.

A third example lies in the mercenary composition of Hellenistic armies. Apart from the Macedonians and Greeks 'proper', these drew on the Greeks of Italy and Sicily and other peoples from that peninsula including a few Romans; they included soldiers from all over the Balkans, Epirus and Illyria and Paeonia and Thrace, and some from the wilder areas north of the Danube; Gauls from Europe and Asia; troops from Africa, from Libya, from Egypt of course, and from the Negro peoples to the far south; and there were Cretans everywhere. There were naturally Syrians and Phoenicians; there were also recruits from all over Asia Minor as far as Pontus and Cappadocia; there were Jews and Arabs; there were Medes and Persians; there were even Indians, skilled in the training of elephants for war. The effect of this was twofold. In the first place it tended to the breakdown of tribal cultures and the acceptance of a common Hellenistic culture within the armed forces. In the second place those who had shared in this common culture tended to take it with them when they retired and returned to their homelands, so that Hellenism spread and became more deeply ingrained. Some might not return; they might make new homes altogether. We know of a number of Greek cities which bestowed their citizenship upon mercenaries who had served them well.

Sculpture is an excellent field in which we can see the new cosmopolis, the diffusion of culture, in action. Gisela Richter in her *Three Critical Periods in Greek Sculpture* (Oxford 1951) has examined the old formula which divided Hellenistic sculpture between 'schools'

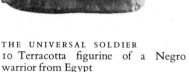

THE UNIVERSAL SOLDIER
10 Terracotta figurine of a Negro
warrior from Egypt

11 Macedonian horseman on a gold
stater of Demetrius Poliorcetes

12 Grave stele of a mercenary soldier
buried at Sidon; his armour and equip-
ment are Greek

– Pergamene, Rhodian, Alexandrian and Mainland – and found it
wanting. A Pergamene style was identified in the tempestuous
gigantomachy. Very good – but the artists who worked on the
gigantomachy came from Athens, and perhaps Tralles and Rhodes, as
well as Pergamum, and the Telephus frieze on the same building is in
a markedly gentler style. So with the other centres. In each we can
trace a variety of styles, in each an international coterie of artists.

Or take the attitude shown by some historians. Before the middle
of the fourth century the majority of historians had confined them-

selves to local history – Antiochus of Syracuse on the Greek colonies of Magna Graecia, Xanthus on Lydia, and innumerable studies called *Persica*, or the fourth-century writers Cleidemus and Androtion on Attic history. By the third quarter of the century the horizons were already receding. Ephorus was the pioneer in universal history and he paved the way for his greater successor Polybius.

One aspect of these expanding horizons was the emergence of cosmopolitan capitals on a different scale from any of the older city-states. The population of these new conurbations might run to several hundred thousand. (In the fourteenth century Milan, Naples, Venice and Florence each had a population of less than 100,000, London less than 50,000.) Such were Antioch and Seleuceia-on-the-Tigris. The largest, and in many ways the symbol of the age, was Alexandria, Alexandria-by-Egypt as it is more properly called.

The city was founded by Alexander – significantly on his return from Siwa – and designed by Deinocrates of Rhodes. Between Lake Mareotis and the sea lay a narrow strip of land, with three-quarters of a mile out a sheltering island. A mole connecting this with the mainland provided a basis for two superb harbours. At the eastern extremity of the island was erected a lighthouse which became one of the wonders of the world; the light from its wood fire, magnified by convex mirrors, was visible thirty miles out to sea, and there were warning sirens worked by steam for bad weather. There may even have been a lift.

The city was planned on a grid-pattern. Canopus Street perhaps followed the line of the old coastal road, but in the new plan was a hundred feet wide and finely paved. At least seven main roads ran parallel to this. Across it was the shorter but similarly mighty Transverse Street with at least ten major roads parallel. The city was divided into five regions known by letters of the Greek alphabet: Alpha, Beta (the palace area), Gamma, Delta (the Jewish quarter), and Epsilon; the exact division has not been identified. Among the great buildings were the palace, Alexander's tomb (known as the Body), the temple of the Muses, the university and library, the zoological gardens, the temple of Sarapis, the magnificent gymnasium, stadium and racecourse, the theatre, the shrine of Pan. A canal was constructed across to the Nile to ensure both communications and the water-supply; the latter was further fostered by rain-water cisterns. A city wall some nine miles long enclosed the site.

13 Detail of the frieze of Telephus from the great altar at Pergamum, showing Telephus and his companions in Mysia

Of all the buildings of Alexandria none was more striking than the temple and sacred enclosure of Sarapis. The foundation plaques discovered in 1943 prove that it was a foundation of Ptolemy III, though there had been a small earlier shrine, and the building was reconstructed on a more lavish scale in Roman times. The result was an impressive citadel; Aphthonius in the early fourth century AD calls it the Acropolis, and Ammianus Marcellinus compares it to the Capitol at Rome. It 'rose into mid-air supported by a mass of constructions' and 'extended in all directions in the form of a square of vast dimensions'. So said the Christian Eunapius, glorying in its overthrow. The temple was destroyed by Christian fanatics in 391, but the foundations resisted even their onslaught.

The Ptolemaic precinct measured 573 × 254 feet. The dedicatory plaques declared:

> King Ptolemy, son of Ptolemy
> and Arsinoe, the Brother-Gods,
> to Sarapis, the temple and precinct.

The building was of limestone, sheathed in painted plaster, including a striking blue tint. One of its early uses was as a daughter library to the great mother library. New heating installations of a Roman type perhaps date from the time when this was expanded with volumes from Pergamum, under Antony and Cleopatra. It was here that Cleopatra, dressed as Isis, received from Antony the captives from the Armenian War. Another accoutrement of the building was the famous Nilometer. Sarapis was not an exclusive god. Like most of the Hellenistic deities, he was accommodating, and we have inscriptions to 'Sarapis and the gods who are with him in the temple'. These certainly included Isis, Harpocrates, who had a shrine dedicated to him by Ptolemy IV, and Hermanoubis, a cross between Horus and Anubis, with some assimilation to Hermes, guide of souls.

Strabo in his own characteristic way takes us round the city. He describes it as shaped like a military cloak, a statement which tells us more about military cloaks than about Alexandria. It is intersected with streets which are practicable for wheeled traffic, two of them being particularly broad. The public precincts and royal palaces are exceptionally handsome, and comprise a quarter to a third of the city; successive kings felt bound to add to the splendour. The gymnasium with its long porticoes is the finest of the public buildings. The shrine of Pan is on an artificial mound ascended by a spiral road, and commands a panorama of the city. Strabo concludes that its greatest natural advantage lies in its site, at the junction of the river traffic brought by the Nile, and the sea traffic, and this makes it the greatest trading centre of the inhabited world.

Alexandria is described in the so-called Potter's Oracle as 'a universal nurse, a city in which every human race had settled'. Strabo called the city 'a universal reservoir'. The ruling class prided themselves on being Greeks, though they were in fact of mixed blood. Polybius puts it well: 'Although of mixed origin, they were in the

14 Bronze coin of Antoninus Pius showing the Serapeum at Alexandria with the famous statue of the god

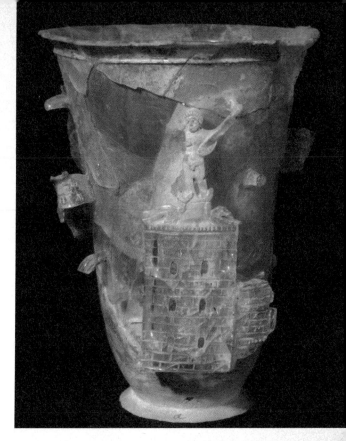

15 Glass vase from Begram, Afghanistan, with a representation of the Pharos at Alexandria

first place Greeks and maintained the general Greek customs.' There was a large Egyptian community, centred on the old village of Rhacotis in the west, but without citizen rights. There was also a large Jewish community with its own concessionary rights. In addition there were communities in smaller numbers from all over the world. John Chrysostom identifies some of them in his day: Greeks, Italians, Syrians, Libyans, Cilicians, Ethiopians, Arabs, Bactrians, Scythians, Indians and Persians. There were others – Thracians and others from Central Europe, Celts from the Balkans and Asia Minor, Phrygians and others from Asia Minor, Carthaginians, Spaniards, Mesopotamians. There must have been few peoples from within range of the eastern Mediterranean who were not represented. The historian Rostovtzeff once said that the Egyptians built an edifice with the native Egyptians in the basement and the foreigners out of the way on the upper floors. The hero of Achilles Tatius' *Clitophon and Leucippe*

25

tells us that the city is bigger than a continent, the population vaster than a nation. One enthusiast declared that Alexandria was the world, the whole earth her territory, the other cities her suburbs.

Theocritus' fifteenth *Idyll* depicts the surging, seething crowds, as Gorgo and Praxinoa go out to the festival.

GORGO: Heavens what a mob! It's ghastly, how can we
get through? There's no end to them – just like ants.

PRAXINOA: Ptolemy, that's one of the best things you've done
since your father went off to the sky. There are no hoods
creeping up as you pass and doing you in – a good
old Egyptian habit.
None of those old tricks, the devils,
all the same, all dirty, all Bolshies –
Gorgo darling, what'll become of us? It's the King's
Own Cavalry. Please, sir, don't run me down.
Look at that bay rearing; he's furious. Eunoa, don't
be a damned fool, get out of the way. . . .

They push their way into the festival. The crush is terrific, like pigs jostling for their swill. Praxinoa gets her cloak torn. But they get in:

PRAXINOA: That's all right. 'All the girls in', as the bridegroom
said when he shut the door.

There is another significant exchange. Someone shushes them for gushing about everything:

PRAXINOA: Hm! Where does he come from? It's none of your
business if we do gush.
We're not your property, you know. We're from
Syracuse and not under your orders.
I'll tell you something else; we're originally from
Corinth,
just like Bellerophon. That's Peloponnesian we're
talking.
I suppose it's all right for Dorians to talk Doric.

In those words we suddenly glimpse the international character of the Alexandrian crowds, the variety of facial and racial types, dresses and accents. Herondas has it too:

Egypt's the very home of Love. Everything,
new and old, is found in Egypt –
riches, sport, power, fine weather, fame,
shows, philosophers, gold, young men,
the shrine of the divine Brother and Sister, the good king,
the Muses' temple, wine, everything your heart desires,
    women. . . .

Lewis Mumford in *The Culture of Cities* (London 1938) saw Alexandria
as an example of Megalopolis and the decline of the city. He identifies
the factors: bigness and power; financial acquisitiveness; aggressive
enterprise; standardization of culture; the triumph of mechanism;
passivity; manual helplessness; bureaucratism; failure of direct
action; scholarship and science by tabulation unrelated to rational
intellectual purpose or social use; domination of education by
encyclopaedic cramming; 'the biggest monuments, the highest
buildings, the most expensive materials, the largest food supply, the
greatest number of worshippers, the biggest population'; exploitation
of the proletariat with occasional philanthropy as an insurance policy;
city life meaning dissociation instead of association; 'life itself com-
partmentalized, dis-specialized, finally disorganized and enfeebled'.

It is of course a generalized picture. His examples are 'Alexandria,
third century B C; Rome, second century A D; Byzantium, tenth
century; Paris, eighteenth century; New York, early twentieth
century'. But the criticism cuts close enough to the bone to be pertinent.
One doubts, however, whether it does justice to the positive side of
Hellenistic Alexandria, the sheer intellectual excitement, the achievement of cosmopolis in miniature.

Cosmopolis needed its own language, and found it in the *koinē*, a
common dialectal form of Greek which became general in the
eastern Mediterranean. Its story can reasonably – though the matter
remains controversial – be traced back to fifth-century Athens. In that
century two things happened: Athens became the predominant
literary centre of the Greek world, and her naval dominion spread
throughout the Aegean and beyond. It was natural that in the fourth
century the influence of Attic should spread and encroach upon other
dialects, and its adoption by Philip of Macedon ensured that Alexander
and the Macedonian generals who became his successors would
continue its dominance. These far-flung kingdoms needed a common

language, and they found it in a modified Attic. The other dialects were not wholly lost. They became absorbed, and Ionic especially was important in moulding the *koinē*. As independent dialects they decayed. Attic forms appear in an inscription from Miletus as early as 450 BC; by the first century the *koinē* has replaced Ionic. Pergamum adopted the *koinē* in the third century. Doric was more tenacious: Dio Chrysostom in the first century AD enjoyed listening to an old woman in the Peloponnese 'with a gentle, attractive Doric accent', and in the following century,' according to Pausanias, the Messenians retained their Doric dialect. But these were exceptional; there was a tendency to standardization through the influence of the capitals, rather like that exercised by Broadcasting House in Britain during the last fifty years.

We need not spend long on technical analysis. The tendency was towards simplification and the elimination of variety. Vowels became assimilated to one another, and the difference between short and long vowels fell away (as in modern Greek), making nonsense of quantitative verse. Diphthongs tended to disappear. So did aspiration. Consonants, too, blurred and blended: *ton logon* became *tollogon*, and the Latin *flagellum* became *phragellion*. The declensions became assimilated to one another; even the forms of genders were confused. Verb-forms were simplified. The indicative encroached on and gradually ousted the subjunctive. And of course vocabulary developed, partly with the natural changes of time, partly with the need for new words to express contemporary concepts. Some of the changes are revealing: *eucharistein* starts by meaning 'do a favour' and ends as 'show gratitude'; *paideuein* from meaning 'educate' comes to mean 'punish'. The Romans were responsible for some adaptations and coinings: words had to be found for consul and prefect, census and province, legion and the rest. So were the Christians. Witness *agapē* for Christian love, a word virtually 'born within the bosom of revealed religion', though the corresponding verb existed before.

The *koinē* was of course the language of the New Testament, and the natural language to express the universalism of the emergent church. They wrote reputable enough Greek, these bilingual Jewish converts. Luke, whose native language may have been Greek, is the finest stylist; the seer of Revelation writes the oddest Greek, but the oddities arise from vigorous individualism rather than from illiteracy.

Cosmopolis needed a new outlook and the philosophies of the

16 Alexandria personified as mistress of the seas on a late Hellenistic mosaic which is probably a copy of an earlier work

Hellenistic age provided it. The change can be seen in the change from Aristotle to his successor Theophrastus. To Aristotle, as we have seen, the 'barbarian', the non-Greek, was by nature a slave. A fragment of Theophrastus shows the concentric circles of kinship within which we live, family, extended family, fellow-citizens, nation or race, human-kind, and lastly the kinship of all living creatures; indeed Theo-phrastus' universalism comes out when in another passage he calls the world 'the common home of gods and men'. The early Cynics had rejected political ties. Diogenes declared himself a citizen of the universe. The attitude was continued by Crates:

> My fatherland has no single tower, no single roof.
> The whole earth is my citadel, a home
> ready for us all to live in.
>
> (Diogenes Laertius)

It was perhaps negative, though this has been overstated by some interpreters. Its positive side is certainly to be seen among the Stoics, though how early it emerged is a matter of controversy.

The Stoics gave the Romans a philosophy of universal empire. The Romans encouraged the Stoic vision. Marcus Aurelius, the half-agnostic Stoic who reached the throne of the world and sat unhappily upon it, brought the two together. 'If intellectual capacity is common to us all, so is Reason, which makes us rational beings. If so, that Reason is common which tells us what to do and what not to do. If so, law is common too. If so, we are citizens. If so, we are fellow-members of a political community. If so, the universe is a kind of city-state. What other political community is there of which we can say that all human beings are fellow-members of it?' Under Rome, too, we find an Epicurean named Diogenes of Oenoanda setting up in public 'the prescription of salvation'. 'We have done this not least for those who are wrongly called foreigners. By the separate divisions of the earth different people acknowledge different fatherlands. But in terms of the whole circle of the universe we all have one single fatherland, the whole earth, and one single home, the universe.' And under Rome Christianity emerged as a universalist religion. We do well not to forget that the Judaism Jesus knew was Hellenistic Judaism, that he grew up in 'Galilee of the Gentiles', that he had a following from the Greek cities of the Decapolis, and that he seems from time to time deliberately to have moved in Gentile territory. Paul, too, came from the Stoic centre of Tarsus, Paul who was to declare that in Christ there were no such things as racial or national differences. In many ways this Hellenized Jew who was also a Roman citizen is a typical representative of the Hellenistic-Roman achievement. Rome turned the whole world (*orbem*) into a single city (*urbem*). Christianity offered the world a new universal religion. Both were nurtured in the soil of Hellenistic cosmopolis.

Cosmopolis did not destroy the polis. It drastically altered the back-cloth against which the polis acted out its drama. It reduced the independence of the polis. But the polis remained and flourished.

Alexander was ultimately responsible for this, too. The Greek cities had retained much of their characteristic quality under the Achaemenid rulers of Persia, partly because they were on the fringes of the Persian empire, partly out of Persian permissive policy, partly through continual interaction with the free cities. When Alexander 'liberated' them he was leading a league of Greek states with himself as president. It is curiously difficult to determine exactly how he handled the liberation, which was for him a major matter of public relations. It seems that he did not in general enrol the liberated cities in the Corinthian League. They had to have autonomy, but they held that autonomy by and at his good pleasure; they might not, for example, take for granted freedom from taxation.

Antigonus went, theoretically, further. On a marble column found at Scepsis and dating from 311 he expressed his concern for Greek freedom, and in outlining the agreement he had just reached with his rivals he recorded: 'We have declared in our treaty that all Greeks shall bind themselves by oath to the mutual defence of their freedom and autonomy.' In fact we know from Diodorus Siculus that Greek autonomy was a part of the treaty agreement and that Antigonus had been foremost in fostering it. No doubt there was policy behind his actions. Still he practised what he preached, and the city of Eresus was allowed to reassert its condemnation of the family of the dictator Agorippus in despite of Antigonus' intervention. So later Antiochus II writes to Erythrae: 'Since Tharsynon, Pythes and Bottas have demonstrated that under Alexander and Antigonus your city was autonomous and exempt from taxes, and since our ancestors were always concerned about its welfare, we, realizing that their policy was just, and anxious not to be behind them in benefactions, will join with you in defence of your autonomy, and agree to your exemption from all taxes including the war-tax against the Gauls.'

The Seleucids in general were notable in the freedom they allowed to the cities. The same policy was overtly followed by the Romans on their intervention in mainland Greece. Flamininus declared at the Isthmian Games in 196 that the cities of Greece were free, without garrisons or tribute, under their ancestral laws. Maybe. But foreign policy was controlled by Rome, and Rome supported the rich and encouraged an increase in the power of the magistrates and council. The relationship between sovereign and city was a difficult and delicate one. Plainly Athens did not enjoy the degree of autonomy which she had exercised in the fifth century; yet some of her fifth-century 'allies' cannot have been much less free under the suzerainty of the Successors than they were as allies of Athens.

Alongside the continuance of the old foundations was the establish-ment of new. Philip had begun this with Philippi, Heraclea Sintica, Philippopolis and other settlements in the Thraceward region. Alexander continued it, and Alexandrias were scattered all over his dominion. Alexandria-by-Egypt is only the best known. Its develop-ment into a massive conurbation was atypical, but its initial character must have been repeated all over the empire. It was a Greek city; the citizens were Greeks or Macedonians, and the indigenous Egyptians were encouraged to settle, but given no political rights. So in Arrian's account Alexander makes the basis for his settlements members of the army who volunteer or who are past further service. The Successors followed suit. Ptolemais in the Thebaid was an autonomous city with its own assembly, council, magistrates and courts. Antigonus founded two cities, one in Bithynia and one in Syria, with settlers from Greece. Seleucus has to his name 16 Antiochs, 9 Seleuceias, 6 Laodiceas, 3 Apameas and a Stratonicea; again we know that he recruited from European Greeks, and that his cities had Greek constitutions. Later, foundations proliferate; the Ptolemies were especially active; but too often now it was merely a renaming of an old town. Tralles we know was at different times called Antioch and Seleuceia. Poor Antigonus was not allowed to leave a name behind him. The various Antigoneias turned into Nicaea or Antioch or Alexandria.

The motives fostering this extension were various. One was habit: the Greeks extended the system familiar to them. One was the desire for glory: city-founders were accorded heroic honours. One was military: new settlements could serve as points of control. Another was economic. Pliny the Elder says that the Macedonian rulers gathered the people of Mesopotamia out of villages into towns 'because of the fertility of the ground'. Similarly in Syria Seleucus I organized the people into townships, and centuries later Ammianus Marcellinus looked on his work with admiration. Polybius comments on the development of the polis in Media.

Recent work has identified some of these remoter settlements. For example a Laodicea has been recognized at Nehavand in Iran, commanding an important route eastwards from the Tigris. Still further east an innominate city has been found on the left bank of the Oxus; the founder was a Thessalian named Cineas, and years later it was visited by Clearchus, presumably the *guru* Clearchus of Soli, who left some moral maxims behind him. In all, the Successors were replacing a half-nomadic village life with settled townships so as to foster the systematic development of agricultural and other resources. Nor should we forget that Pergamum, Sardis and Tarsus were transformed native settlements.

The original Greek element in many of these cities was relatively small, and new foundations must often have drawn on the local population for their womenfolk. The term 'half-foreign' (*mixobarbaros*) used of Antioch must have had a much wider application. At Dura-Europos the population was hardly Greek at all; the original settlers were Macedonian, and they retained their northern institutions. Here, too, they intermarried with the local population. But despite the absence of the usual civic pattern, Dura-Europos was a recognizable polis. Some cities received a shot in the arm from fresh Greek immigration. On one inscription yet another Antioch, on the Persian Gulf, thanks Magnesia-on-the-Maeander for 'a large number of admirable men' who settled there, no doubt with their families. The general pattern was of a Greek ruling class, a free population from the locality to engage in the practical business of economic production, and a substructure of slavery. It is curiously Platonic.

New foundations and new developments were scientifically planned. The principles went back to Hippodamus of Miletus in the fifth century. Priene, refounded in Alexander's reign, offers a good example; it shows on a small scale (the population was about four thousand) just what a polis meant physically. The site is hilly, but despite this the streets are aligned strictly north–south and east–west. The agora, or city centre and central market, lies off the main east–

west street. The plan allows for blocks of about 155 × 116 feet, each comprising four larger houses or eight smaller houses, well built, with lofty rooms and inner courts. The public buildings follow the basic pattern and occupy one or more blocks. The whole is surrounded by an irregular wall which is designed for military efficiency. It follows the line of optimum defensibility, and encloses a considerable area of unusable ground; it is sturdily constructed and founded on rock. Dura-Europos on the Euphrates is closely similar, except that the blocks are somewhat larger – about 328 × 131 feet. The impression is of a life which was at once rationally ordered and vigorously prosperous.

New developments came with the rise of Pergamum and might be called the triumph of the stoa. The Pergamene architects devised a new form of stoa with two storeys, the lower Doric, the upper Ionic, each with a Doric entablature. The invention was not wholly successful aesthetically, as these architects were conservative in making the proportion approximate to those of the two stages of a Doric temple, and the upper seems displeasingly small. A balcony or balustrade ran along the upper storey. Furthermore, the exigencies and opportunities provided by sloping sites led to elaborate basements. Aegae, Alinda and Assos all offer good examples. The new pattern of stoa can be well seen in the reconstructed Stoa of Attalus in the agora at Athens, given to the city by Attalus II who had studied for a period at the Academy. It has a colonnade of forty-five columns, Doric below and Ionic above as usual, with twenty-one shops at the back and a staircase at each end. The building also contains the first known use of a visible arch in Athenian architecture. These great stoas served a double function. They provided the shade so necessary in a sun-drenched climate, and at the same time made a convenient shopping centre. There are modern parallels, except that the shelter, in Britain at least, is from the traffic rather than from the sun.

Hellenization spread to cities which were not in origin Greek. Their very names were Hellenized. Pella in the Decapolis had a Semitic name near enough to that of the Macedonian capital; similarly (we may suspect) 'Ain Teda became Anthedon. Semitic deities were identified with the Greek pantheon: so Baalbek became Heliopolis and Arsuf Apollonia. Legendary links were established: Iconium claimed Perseus, Selge Calchas, Antioch Triptolemus. Greek magistrates are found in the remoter regions of Asia Minor, and the variety of titles which they bear, *demiourgos, prytanis, stephanephoros, strategos* and the like, strongly suggests that this was a matter of local initiative rather than imperial policy on the part of the Seleucids. Coins were issued on Greek models with Greek inscriptions. Greek literature, art and architecture spread: even the Jews had buildings after the Greek pattern. Nacrusa in northern Lydia had a Greek constitution by the middle of the third century; by the end of the century Delphi had actually acknowledged the old Lydian capital of Sardis as a Greek city.

The Classical Greek city normally confined its citizenship to children whose parents were both citizens. This remained the basis in the Hellenistic age, but the ties were looser. For example, when Miletus absorbed Pedasa, it accepted the citizens of Pedasa as citizens of Miletus. Rhodes followed a similar policy towards the towns it acquired in Asia Minor. Again, reciprocal citizen rights were not uncommon; we have surviving treaties between Miletus and some of the city-states in the vicinity; a citizen of the latter resident in Miletus acquired Milesian citizenship, and *vice versa*. (Thomas Jefferson thought that some such scheme between modern nation-states might form a basis for world peace.) Individual benefactors were in increasing numbers granted the citizenship of the states which they benefited: we have noticed this with mercenaries, but it was by no means confined to them.

The internal constitution was in general democratic, within the Greek meaning of that word: that is to say that attempts to restrict the number of adult male citizens who might participate in the affairs of state, and to confine power to an unrepresentative clique, failed. Antipater tried it, and so did Cassander; but they soon found their support falling away before the more popular policies of Antigonus. The Ptolemies were more successfully oligarchical, and at Cyrene political power was limited to a theoretical ten thousand, with an economic qualification, though this figure was a compromise and far less limited than the local oligarchs would have wished. Even under Roman rule, when power had passed to the council and the magistrates, Plutarch thinks it important to advise a budding statesman in ways of influencing the assembly.

The council controlled the exercise of democracy by controlling the business of the assembly. It was, however, a representative body, and its members served for a limited period, normally a year; Cyrene had a sensible device for ensuring continuity whereby members of the

17 The *bouleuterion* (council chamber) at Priene, where traditional city-state institutions were preserved in a setting of rationalistic town planning

council served for two years, half of them retiring in alternate years. The normal formula in legislation runs, 'It was decided by council and people.'

The magistrates were generally elected; the Athenian system of appointment by lot did not commend itself. (Some priesthoods naturally remained hereditary.) Tenure of office was normally limited, most commonly to a year, but in some states including Rhodes the period was six months, and in Chalcedon and Erythrae it was actually

18 The theatre at Pergamum, a prosperous cultural centre ruled by kings but retaining the constitution of a polis

confined to four months. Magistrates were subject to investigation at the close of their period of office. A further check lay in the fact that the more important offices were collegiate. Responsibility either rotated among the members of the board, or was exercised corporately.

But though in theory office was open to any citizen, the evidence is quite clear that it tended to be confined to the wealthy; in some financial offices there was a property qualification as a precaution against corruption. In Classical Athens a 'liturgy' of compulsory expenditure on behalf of the state might be laid upon rich citizens. Demetrius of Phalerum abolished this system. But in consequence magistrates were expected to contribute 'voluntarily' to the benefit of their fellow-citizens, and this meant in effect that only the rich could afford to be magistrates; there is in fact an inscription decreeing that citizens of Medeon who have already held office there, shall not, if they exercise their right of double citizenship with Stiris, be compelled to 'perform the liturgy of a magistracy' in that city as well. Similarly a long inscription from Eleusis, dating from the end of the third century, commends Demaenetus for the generosity of his liturgies while in office.

One of the features of political reality in the Hellenistic age was naturally that freedom in international relations was circumscribed. The cities might be nominally autonomous, but in the last resort they were items in a wider dominion. The result of this was a greater concentration on internal politics. The office of *strategos* or 'general', which was closely associated with military affairs and foreign policy, lost its absolute pre-eminence, and the gymnasiarch and *agoranomus*, concerned with education and economics, attained greater significance.

Liaison between the cities was encouraged by the kings as a matter of policy. Philip started it with his League of Corinth of which he himself was president (*hegemon*); this comprised all the states of Greece except Sparta. There was no common citizenship. It was in fact little more than a co-ordination of the city-states in a common relationship with the president to allow him to dictate foreign policy. Alexander succeeded to Philip's position, and in the revived League of 302 we find the formula, 'the king and the Greeks'. Leagues allowed a monarch to make his wishes – courteously but firmly – known to more than one state at the same time. Sometimes he would push in his own nominee to a position of authority as a means of control. A good example is the League of the Islanders, with its religious centre in Delos, a citizenship common to all the islands, but political dependence on whichever of the monarchs happened to dominate the Aegean, and its highest official a non-islander and the monarch's nominee. Another example is the revived Ionian League, to which Lysimachus appointed the *strategos*.

But we must not think of the leagues as mere pawns of imperial policy. There were also leagues which were genuine political experiments and rose out of the natural and fruitful development of the city-state. Confederacies of varying degrees of stringency had existed in the Classical period. In the third century there were numerous confederacies, some of long standing. In Boeotia a confederacy in which the magistrates had been dominated by Thebes and the primary assembly had operated by the right of all citizens to vote (giving the power to the largest city – Thebes) modified its system so that the magistrates were chosen one from each constituent member-state, and the assembly voted city by city. In Aetolia there was a confederacy with a strong primary assembly, meeting twice a year, and a council with proportional representation of the member-states. An interesting feature was the existence of tribal districts between the cities and the whole confederacy. Their neighbours in Acarnania also had a federal constitution. The two confederacies were generally hostile, but at one point in the third century they did actually agree on mutual rights of citizenship.

Among all the confederacies none is more interesting than the Lycian. Here in the wilds of the mountains of Asia Minor a non-Greek people developed under Greek influence a federal constitution which by 100 B C had moved so far in the direction of representative government that they did away with the primary assembly altogether. Representation was in approximate proportion to population: a city might have one, two or three representatives on the council and proportionately more in the assembly – such at least is a reasonable interpretation of the evidence. The Lycian confederacy survived well into the Roman Empire, though its powers of action were severely circumscribed.

The best-known and most studied of the confederacies is the Achaean League. It had existed earlier. According to Polybius, the Achaeans passed directly from a unitary monarchy to a federal republic; he may be right, for it was his home territory. We have no certain knowledge of the institutions, but the concept of federal citizenship had begun to emerge and non-Achaeans were actually admitted. The old League collapsed shortly after 300, to be revived in 281–280. The initiative came from the coastal towns of Dyme and Patrae. Tritaea and Pherae joined them. Aegium next threw off Macedonian overlordship and joined. The confederacy was now strong enough to intervene in other cities. They got rid of the dictator in power at Bura, and won the city. At Cerynea the dictator read the writing on the wall, abdicated, and brought the city in. 'For the first

19 Coin of the original Achaean League, showing the head of Artemis and Zeus enthroned

twenty-five years', wrote Polybius, 'the above-mentioned cities shared in a confederacy, appointed a common secretary according to a rota, and two generals. After that they took a fresh decision to appoint a single general, and to entrust him with plenary authority. Margus of Cerynea was the first.' In addition, as we know from inscriptional evidence, there were ten magistrates called *demiourgoi*. After the accession of Aegium they met at the nearby shrine of Zeus Hamarios, their patron deity; subsequently meetings were transferred to the city assembly.

Then in 251 Aratus, one of the dominant figures of Greek politics, rid his native Sicyon of its dictator and brought it into the League. Sicyon was not an Achaean city, and Aratus' view was a wider one than that of his new confederates. By 245 he was elected general; he held office regularly in alternate years, and was the major figure in determining policy without alternation. Aratus was a liberator; he loathed dictators, and he loathed the autocratic power of Macedon. He won the League to the work of liberation. He was himself a notable guerilla leader: in some ways he seems like a twentieth-century figure of the Third World. In 243 he liberated Corinth. The accession was prestigious. Megara followed freely: so did some of the towns of the Argolid. At Argos itself, and at Athens, he failed. At Sparta economic revolution and resurgent nationalism defied him. Aratus was no radical. He disliked both movements. Cleomenes of Sparta won Argos where Aratus had failed. He then won Corinth from Aratus. The confederacy was shrinking.

The clash between the two great Greeks of the time was tragic. Aratus, incorruptible, adventurous, persuasive, skilled in diplomacy, passionately attached to freedom and implacably ambitious for his own position, stood for federalism without social revolution, Cleomenes for social revolution mingled with pride in Spartan nationalism.

Aratus had spent his life fighting for federalism and freedom against the Macedonian imperialists. Now, challenged by a new power from the south, he preferred to sell his life's work back to the imperialists rather than see it destroyed by Cleomenes' revolution. He surrendered federalism and freedom to fear, and called in Macedon. Even the brilliance of Cleomenes could not withstand the armoured divisions from the north. In 222 BC he fought and lost. Aratus' federation was allowed to retain an illusory freedom; it was in fact a mere pawn in Macedonian policy. Aratus was permitted to continue playing at politics, subject to Macedonian approval. 'The republican chief had stooped to become a courtier and a Minister.' He was no doubt a suave courtier and a wise minister, but in breaking Cleomenes' revolution he had broken his own power.

Yet even now the significance of the League was not over. During the period of which we have been speaking the confederacy took its decisions through a primary assembly, seemingly open to all citizens over thirty. Subsequently the primary assembly met only when summoned for an extraordinary general meeting, and executive decision was vested in the council, who even elected the magistrates. The council was no doubt large; how large we do not know, but probably several hundred strong. To all intents and purposes this was the establishment of representative government. Meetings of the assembly were few, and for that reason attended with some pomp and circumstance. The agenda was limited to a single previously announced item. The session lasted for three days. The first was spent in introducing the issues; the second was used for debate; the third was for voting. It was the assembly which took the decision to back Rome rather than Macedon; but it was the council which rejected overtures from Eumenes of Pergamum.

E. A. Freeman, great historian that he was, singled out four federal commonwealths as commanding supremely the attention of students of political history: the Achaean League (281–146 BC), the Swiss Cantons from the thirteenth century to his own day, the United Provinces of the Netherlands (AD 1571–1795), and the United States from 1778 to his own day. What the Achaean League did, over a limited area and for a limited period, was to combine the distinctive quality of the polis with a wider vision. The coins of the League show devotion to Zeus Homagyrius and Demeter Panachaea, and Aphrodite in Corinth and Hera in Argos actually yield to these overarching

20 Figurine of a slave and a boy reading

powers. Just as the United States has become a 'maxi-state', so Polybius claimed that at the height of the Achaean League the whole Peloponnese could be thought of as a single polis. (See map, p. 162.)

The prosperity of the polis did not end with the coming of Rome. On the contrary it is arguable that the early Roman Empire was its great period. Pompey had founded some new cities over towards the Black Sea; one was called Pompeiopolis. Caesar and Augustus established a number of Roman colonies in the East, either as a relief to land-hunger in Italy or for the settlement of veteran soldiers. Many of the veterans were already Greek-speaking, and it is interesting to watch how Greek ousts Latin within the colonies. But most imperial foundations were in fact Greek cities. Some of these were the establishment of a polis where there had formerly been villages, the synoecism of earlier Greek history. Sebaste in the valley of the Senarus is one example, Neapolis in Samian territory, a foundation of Antoninus Pius, another, and, on a grander scale, Nicopolis a third.

This is important. The secret of Roman government lay largely in the development of the *municipium*. It lay in the double loyalty, which, as we have seen, increasingly took the form of a double citizenship. Rome conquered by force, but ruled by consent. The vast spread of North Africa from Morocco to the borders of Egypt was policed by a single legion based on Lambaesis. This would scarcely have been possible with a dissatisfied population. Satisfaction arose quite largely from the combination of a world authority, to which local citizens all over the world might aspire to belong, exercising a providential government, with an intense sense of local 'belonging' and genuine responsibility exercised in a recognizable neighbourhood. This the *municipium* provided. Its model was the polis.

The political achievement of the polis in the Hellenistic age, then, was to retain effective local government in significant independence of the distant monarchs. Civic loyalty was strong and remained strong, and this in the end was the political mainspring of society. Alongside this is the cultural achievement; we should not forget that Tacitus saw Seleuceia-on-the-Tigris as an outpost of civilization resisting foreign influence. Civic patriotism formed an equal outlet here. Of course the great visible demonstrative examples of culture were provided by patronage from rich citizens or from the rulers' courts. But even there we should not underestimate the power of local loyalty: witness the benefactions of Herodes Atticus or the Epicurean inscription of Diogenes of Oenoanda. Physical fitness was encouraged; the gymnasium and palaestra were standard features of the Greek city. So was the theatre; and the guild of Dionysus was supported by state expenditure. State funds also fostered higher education. So did private benefaction: witness the gifts of Eudemus at Miletus, or Polythrous at Teos; the latter gave no less than 34,000 drachmae.

Interest in education was widespread. Travelling lecturers and preachers, whether Cynic, or, later, Christian, could command wide audiences. Many did travel, and yet retained their local roots; even in Roman times we speak naturally of Apollonius of Tyana, or Lucian of Samosata. Indeed, to mention literary figures of the Hellenistic and Graeco-Roman periods is to remind ourselves how various were the cities from which they came – Poseidonius of Apamea, Leonidas of Tarentum, Meleager of Gadara (which also produced Philodemus), Philitas of Cos, Antimachus of Colophon, Zeno of Citium (founder of the Stoics), Zeno of Tarsus (a later Stoic: Tarsus also produced Paul), Zeno of Sidon (an Epicurean), Strabo of Amaseia, Callimachus of Cyrene, Pytheas of Marseilles – the list could be extended almost indefinitely. Plutarch of Chaeronea is a magnificent example of local loyalty. He was a man of considerable culture; he visited Rome and Alexandria; he was listened to and respected by the imperial authorities. But his life was spent in and devoted to Chaeronea. Such is the power of the polis.

III WAYS AND MEANS

One obvious economic change in the Hellenistic age is the extension of the trade routes. Now for the first time there was trade with China, and the trade with East Africa, Arabia and India was immeasurably developed. The Egyptian trade was mainly by sea, and the port of Berenice on the Red Sea was of considerable importance. The discovery of the monsoon in the late second century greatly facilitated this. Coptos on the Upper Nile became a key centre. But the Egyptians were interested in the Asiatic transcontinental traffic as well, and for this reason were concerned about the possession of the ports of Palestine.

The great route through the Seleucid empire ran from Seleuceia-on-the-Tigris to Antioch-on-the-Orontes; branches led to Ephesus and Damascus. Seleuceia communicated with India by the Tigris and a sea route, by a minor land route through Susa and Persepolis, and by a major land route through Ecbatana (Hamadan), and Bactra (Balkh) to Taxila. Dura-Europos was an early Seleucid military colony on the Euphrates protecting the lines of trade. Petra flourished as the Nabataean capital: when the future Dean Burgon in an undergraduate poem described it as

A rose-red city half as old as time

he meant literally that its history extended halfway back to 4004 B C, but its greatest prosperity began in 312; it commanded the inland routes from Tyre and Gaza. Towards the end of the period the old Aramaic town of Tadmor, now known as Palmyra, captured control of the trade; at the western side of the desert we begin to hear of the Decapolis, the League of Ten Cities, first mentioned in the New Testament. At the other end there was a sea route from Mesopotamia to India, and land routes to India and China. Alexander's foundation of Heratus was a key point. The advance of Chinese military power from Turkestan at the end of the second century fostered this trade. Imports from China included silk and other textiles, bamboo and iron.

Among exports were plants and trees of several varieties (including vines), woollen goods, olives, wine, and art work of various kinds which even had a stylistic effect on Chinese art. Nor should we forget the extension of routes in the other direction: Pytheas of Marseilles at the end of the fourth century passing through the Straits of Gibraltar, circumnavigating Britain, seemingly reaching Norway and the Elbe, and the consequent development of the tin trade with Cornwall; Eudoxus of Cyzicus, turning south out of the Straits and seeking to circumnavigate Africa.

Trade within the Mediterranean basin was mainly in essentials, or things regarded as essentials. Metals came first. Many of the old veins, like the Athenian silver mines at Laurium, were worked out. Silver now came predominantly from Spain, and copper from Cyprus, which was safely in Ptolemaic hands. Iron was widespread, but the best quality came from the south shores of the Black Sea; later, Chinese iron was in demand. Tin, as we have seen, came from outside also, from Cornwall. Food was the next important item of trade. Corn was exported from Egypt, North Africa and the Crimea; perhaps also from Babylonia. Local wine was available everywhere; high-quality wine from Syria, Asia Minor and the islands was in demand. Some areas had their specialities. Athens specialized in olive oil and honey, Byzantium in fish, Jericho in dates, Damascus in prunes. Trade in textiles came third: linen from Egypt, woollen goods from Miletus and elsewhere. Timber came from Macedon and the north; the Seleucids had the forests of Asia Minor; Egypt drew on supplies from the Lebanon. Building marble came from Paros and Athens, granite from Egypt; some docks constructed in Delos about 130 BC are of Egyptian granite. The more distant traffic was mainly in luxury goods: ivory from India and Africa south of the Sahara; precious stones and spices from Arabia and India. Naturally middlemen took advantage of trade. Two of the most prosperous centres of the eastern Mediterranean, Rhodes and Delos (which the Romans backed as a rival to Rhodes), had little to offer themselves, and flourished on the transit trade.

Money is the basis of any complex economy. One result of the spread of cosmopolis was the development of common standards of currency. Philip had already adopted the Attic standard for gold; Alexander adopted it for silver also, and all the Successors followed suit except for the Ptolemies, who preferred the Phoenician standard.

These two prevailed throughout the Hellenistic world. Local currencies with their own standards remained, in Rhodes for example, or in some of the mainland federations, but they were of minor importance by comparison. The only serious challenge to the Attic and Phoenician standards came from Rome. Exactly how early the pressures from Rome built up is a matter of some controversy, but by the latter part of the first century BC her triumph was complete.

The natural effect of Alexander's conquest of the East was to decrease the rarity of gold: it was equally natural that gold should increase in value during the centuries which followed, especially as the opening of silver mines in Spain made silver more plentiful. The ratio of silver to gold during this period oscillated between about 1:10 and 1:15; that of copper to silver fluctuated, sometimes violently, around 1:120. But the most serious examples of inflation and currency crisis were confined to Egypt, where the first major crisis began about 220 BC.

Interest is another index of the monetary economy. In the fourth century it was regularly at 12 per cent, except in Delos, which kept the rate down to 10 per cent. By 300 BC the rate was generally down to 10 per cent except in the outlying areas of the new states, where the demand for capital pushed it up as high as 24 per cent; in 282 Miletus was allowed a 6 per cent loan, but this was as a special favour. By the second century rates had come down, and varied between about 5 per cent and 10 per cent.

Greece itself was for the most part in decline, though there were for a brief period rising standards about 260 BC. We have evidence of unemployment, falling wages, poverty, land reverting to wilderness even in areas as potentially productive as Euboea and Thessaly, deforestation and shortage of timber, the swallowing of smallholdings by large estates which were themselves underdeveloped, emigration and depopulation. There were small pockets of prosperity, as at Tanagra which flourished on the production of figurines, but these are exceptional. The centres of Hellenic prosperity had moved with the movement of Hellenism, from Athens to Alexandria, from Corinth to Rhodes, from Sparta to Pergamum, from Argos to Antioch.

Athens, about which we know most, at first enjoyed renewed prosperity. The 'West Slope' ware and the new relief vases are found as far afield as Russia and Egypt, and a new building programme was sponsored. It did not last. The circulation of Persian gold led to

CULTURAL DIFFUSION

21 Bronze statuette of a parrot, from Samsun in Asia Minor

22 Fragment of woollen tapestry found in a grave pit at Lou-Lan in China

23 Mirror with silver-gilt border unearthed at Olbia in southern Russia

24 A repoussé silver pot showing fishermen, from Egypt

25 Athenian 'West Slope' ware, c. 300 B C

inflated prices. The mines at Laurium seem to have gone out of business, and the abandonment of silver coinage in 261 was a severe setback to prosperity and prestige. Macedonian domination loosened the economic structure. The balance of trade changed adversely; in the latter half of the third century the main export, oil, fell in price, and the main import, grain, rose. Heracleides said that Athens was the most delightful place in the world, provided you brought your own food. The wages of the urban workers fell; the Egyptian peasant was better remunerated. There was emigration, especially but not exclusively to Egypt. Rival centres, as we have seen, challenged and destroyed Athenian dominance.

The restoration of independence in 229 improved the situation. Grain came from Pontus and Egypt, wine from the islands, perfumes from the East through Syria; exports were oil, honey and vases of clay and silver. The Laurium mines were opened up again, and the New Style coinage proved popular and won the confidence of Greece. The extent of trading contacts is revealed by inscriptions: there were resident traders from all over the Aegean, from the Black Sea, Palestine and Egypt, and a few from Italy and Sicily. The acquisition of Delos brought economic benefit to Athens; Poseidonius records an Athenian of uncertain name who made his fortune on the island. The Parthenon was restored after a fire, the Piraeus theatre restored, the agora immensely developed.

Yet all was not really well. In 172–171 BC a special fund had to be raised to repair fortifications in the Piraeus. Benefactions were coming from the monarchs overseas: the Stoa of Attalus is an obvious example; Antiochus Epiphanes put up money for the temple of Zeus Olympius; and we have records of gratitude to a number of queens, Nysa of Cappadocia, Stratonice of Pergamum, Nysa of Pontus, for unknown benefactions. At home there was social unrest. We know of two slave revolts, in 130 BC and 103 BC. The curious events which preceded Sulla's sacking of the city suggest economic and political discontent: the courts deprived of the right to hold magistrates accountable, the right-wing Medeius holding office for three successive years, restrictions on freedom of expression and public assembly, the brief dictatorship of Athenion by appeal to the poorer classes, the proscription of the rich and confiscation of property, and the alignment with Mithradates against Rome. Even with the confiscations, which included money from Delos, Sulla could loot only forty pounds of gold and

26 Limestone grave monument showing strong Greek influence, from Ptolemaic Egypt

27 Bronze herm signed by Boethus of Chalcedon, recovered from a wreck off Mahdia on the Tunisian coast

28 Figure of a Garunda found near Jalalabad, Afghanistan; the sculptor was an Indian of the Graeco-Buddhist (Gandara) school, which flourished between 50 BC and AD 150

six hundred pounds of silver. It is a sure sign of the economic decline; the rich may have been relatively rich, but the whole economy was in decay.

It is not surprising in these conditions that there was a demand for economic revolution. The haves were afraid of the have-nots. Early in the third century Praxicles of Naxos lent three talents to the city of Acesine in Amorgos; as a condition of the loan the city mortgaged all its own property as well as the property of citizens and of resident aliens (metics). This last shows that Praxicles was afraid of a revolution which might lead to the failure to honour financial obligations.

In Sparta, Agis IV essayed economic and social reforms on a basis of land nationalization; he failed and was murdered. Young Cleomenes III went further. He abolished the power of the aristocrats and produced a state of equality under the monarchy. He abolished debts (nearly always owed by poor farmers to capitalist landlords), redistributed the land, and in general espoused a communistic economic revolution. He restored the common meals, ancient simplicity of life and education for character traditional among the Spartans.

From Sparta the ideas spread to the rest of Greece. Cleomenes had turned a dream into a reality. The fire of revolution swept through the dry forest of cities long parched for justice. Everywhere were demands for 'division of land and cancellation of debts'. At Megalopolis, Cercidas, who contrived to be at once a Cynic and an aristocrat, is found preaching philanthropy and exhorting his fellow-aristocrats to heal the sick and give to the poor before it is too late and the revolution is upon them.

Turn the greedy cormorant to poverty.
Give to us the riches uselessly wasted.
Ask God Almighty; when the rich set their hearts
on nothing but money, God should take away their swinish
    wealth.
Give to the frugal, who drink from a common bowl,
the money he squanders on extravagances. Is justice blind?
The sun unseeing? Righteousness bleary-eyed? Vengeance is
    coming
and Victory. Storms will overwhelm the rich, the proud.
Once swallowed, the whirlpool will never vomit them up
    again.

It reads like a prophecy from the Book of Amos. In Boeotia debts were practically cancelled and the historian Polybius blames a man named Opheltas for using state funds to help the poor. But Cleomenes, as we have seen, fell foul of Aratus, was beaten down by Macedon, and saw his work undone. He retired to Egypt, where he committed suicide after a last unsuccessful attempt to raise the flag of social justice in Alexandria.

Revolutionary movements were particularly strong between 138 and 122 BC, and they were not confined to Greece. There were two reasons for this – a succession of bad harvests, and turbulence in Central Asia caused by nomadic tribes. In Rome itself there was a slave rising, as well as the disturbances associated with the Gracchi and arising from economic hardship. At Minturnae and Sinuessa severe reprisals imply a mood of fear. In Sicily a Syrian priest named Eunus fostered a revolutionary insurgence. It is a revealing fact that the slaves behaved with exemplary discipline, but there was looting and direct action by the poor against the rich. In Pergamum Aristonicus challenged the bequest to Rome with the support of slaves and the group one is tempted to call 'poor whites'. In Delos and elsewhere there were slave revolts. In Attica and Macedonia the brutally exploited miners rose. We have the impression of intolerable economic hardship behind these risings, which were suppressed by the superior power of Rome.

The areas of agricultural prosperity lay in Egypt and Asia. Egypt, 'the gift of the Nile', had long possessed, and was to retain, agricultural prosperity; this was the period when it really became established as the granary of the ancient world. Cereals included wheat, barley and sorghum; flax was of major importance; the land was rich in vegetables, lentils, beans, chickpea and onions; there was no olive culture, but the the palm prospered and other fruits flourished; there was also papyrus. Animals too – horses and donkeys, goats and cattle, as well as poultry; and of course there was ample fishing.

Egypt, with its immense resources, used a system of state capitalism. The state owned a large part of the land – in one locality where we happen to have information, over half – and the rest was liable to taxation; even gift estates involved obligations as well as privileges. The state also owned large areas of industrial enterprise in mines, quarries, fisheries and factories. Ownership extended even to forests in Cyprus and the Lebanon. There was indirect control through the state banking system, and through stocks of grain and tools which had to be rented from the state. There was heavy taxation on imports. In some goods, notably oil, there was a state monopoly, and this applied to papyrus too, which to all intents grew only in Egypt, and provided a profitable export. There was extensive control of the food supply, of basic necessities such as clothing, and of some luxury goods. The result was enormous prosperity at the centre, while the workers remained near the bread-line and were subject to continual impositions, inventories and inspections. Claire Préaux has compared the Ptolemaic economy with the fiscality of France at the end of the Ancien Régime. The astonishing thing is that before the coming of the Greeks Egypt was very much a Stone Age state: successive metallic revolutions had passed it by. The new order was a change indeed.

It was Ptolemy II who restored the economic life of Egypt through his minister of economics, Apollonius, and the latter's business executive, Zeno; detailed records of their work around Philadelphia in the Fayum have survived, and show interests extending widely in Egypt (with properties in Alexandria and Memphis), as well as a merchant fleet making possible trade in the eastern Mediterranean. The estate at Philadelphia covered about three square miles, the equivalent of a thousand normal holdings. It was reclaimed land. Its development involved the draining of marshland, the construction of dykes and the irrigation of sandy soil: among our papyrus records is a chart showing dykes and canals. Brushwood and reeds had to be cleared, the vine and other plants introduced, methods of cultivation improved. Animal husbandry was developed with improved stocks. A building programme was instituted, expanding the hamlet of Philadelphia into a large village. Modern methods of administration were applied and the agriculture systematized. The produce was varied. In addition to livestock there were cereals, though these were not very lucrative, oil-plants, vines, orchards, market gardens, garlic, and honey.

Strabo is an excellent source for the prosperity of Asia from the coast to Mesopotamia and beyond. Thus, on Babylonia he writes: 'No other country produces such crops of barley; its yield is said to be three hundredfold. For the rest the palm tree supplies everything – bread, wine, vinegar, honey, meal, all the material for weaving, combustible material from the date-stones, which are also soaked in water and given as food to farm animals. For oil they use sesame. . . . Babylonia also produces asphalt in great quantities.' Mesopotamia generally is 'good pasture-land, and rich in vegetation, evergreens and spice'.

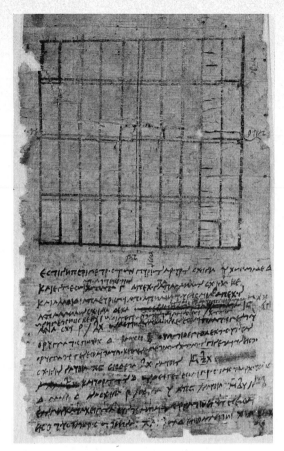

29 Chart of a
Ptolemaic irrigation
scheme, dating
from the reign of
Ptolemy II

Samosata is surrounded by a 'small but exceptionally fertile belt of land'. Apamea is 'richly endowed with a wide belt of fertile land'; the meadows of the Orontes provide pasture for cattle and horses. South Arabia is 'generally fruitful, and particularly good for honey'. It does not support horses, mules or pigs, but there are plenty of other farm animals; and there are no geese or chickens but all kinds of other birds. The country round Susa is so rich in grain that the yield is a hundred-fold or more. The Greeks introduced the vine there, as in South Arabia. Sometimes the process was in the other direction. Rice came westwards from India into Iran, Mesopotamia and Lower Syria.

Or again, look at Strabo's evidence on Asia Minor. The whole of Melitene (a region of Cappadocia) is planted with fruit trees; the olive

53

30 Roman terracotta frieze depicting scenes of Egyptian agricultural life

prospers, and they produce a wine which stands comparison with the
best wines of Greece. Cataonia is a broad plain set in a basin and
produces everything except evergreens. The area around Mazaca is
not obviously attractive for habitation, but its resources in stone and
timber have been developed for building, and there is good cattle-
grazing. In general Cappadocia is excellent orchard country, cornland
and grazing-ground. Its mineral resources include red ochre, crystal,
onyx and a form of mica; Strabo incidentally reveals the development
of trade routes by mentioning that in earlier times the Cappadocians
exported through Sinope on the Black Sea, but later developed
another route to Ephesus. Again, in Pontus, Strabo has a lucent
account of the prosperity of Sinope with its fine walls and splendid
buildings, and the market gardening in the suburbs and environs.
Further out from the city is an area of intensive olive cultivation, and
on the mountains timber for shipbuilding and furniture. The adjoining district to the east is flat and fertile, and has a prosperous wool
industry. Further east again is the well-watered plain of Themiscyra,
with pasture for cattle and horses and virtually unlimited crops of
millet and sorghum. The mountains abound in wild fruits and con-
sequently in wild animals. Strabo implies that they could have been
developed for farming, but they offered so much in their natural state

that it was not worth while. Further along again is mining country, so effectively developed that the veins of silver are exhausted, though resources in iron remain. Industrialization has replaced agriculture, but a large fishing industry remains. Or, if we move inland, immediately south of Themiscyra lies Phanaroea, the most prosperous area of Pontus, excellent for vine and olive and with many other qualities. Mithradates developed a palace here, with zoological gardens, hunting grounds, and some industry represented by mines and a famous water-mill. The adjoining territory is fertile in grain, and has good pasture-land and a lake with a fishing industry.

Pass to Bithynia, and we note the development of cattle and cheese. Galatia is wilder; some of it is suitable only for grazing asses, but prosperous sheep-farming has been developed on unpromising terrain. Pisidia has developed the olive. Strabo has an eloquent description of Selge, high in the Taurus mountains, with its prosperous population and ordered government. The country around grows olives and vines; it is good pasture-land and also offers timber forests. One of the trees is a gum-tree called *styrax*; the wood is good for spears, and the gum is released by a wood-boring beetle. Laodicea in Phrygia, the Laodicea which is condemned for indifference by the seer of Patmos, has a superb wool, soft and black; so does nearby Colossae where the wool is dyed purple.

Needless to continue. Strabo describes his own city of Amaseia as admirably devised by nature and human foresight. Possibly. But the gardener who answered the vicar's comment, 'The Almighty has used you as his fellow-worker in producing a beautiful garden', with, 'You should have seen what it was like when the Almighty had it all to himself', had a point, and the present wild desolation of some of these once prosperous regions shows what the Hellenistic monarchies achieved.

State expenditure was large. The military estimates then as now swallowed up a formidable share of the budget. More constructive public works were also a burden on the royal exchequer: notably flood control and irrigation in Mesopotamia and Egypt. The new city foundations cost money. The patronage of education, science and the arts, especially in Alexandria and Pergamum, must have been proportionately comparable with modern public expenditure on higher education and the arts. The courts themselves were luxurious and expensive, especially under the Ptolemies and Seleucids.

Among the works attributed to Aristotle is a treatise entitled *Economics*. The second book, which dates from some time in the third century and is certainly not by Aristotle, is little more than a series of anecdotes on the fund-raising exploits of various authorities, including the early Hellenistic monarchs and their representatives. Royal economic authority, while theoretically unlimited, can be analysed into four heads: currency (including price regulation), imports, exports, and expenditure (both sides of the budget). Revenue is in fact left to the provincial governors, and falls under six heads: agricultural revenue (a tithe on land produce), revenue from local mineral resources, revenue from markets, revenue from taxes on land and sales, revenue from animal produce (again a tithe), and other sources, poll-tax, or an industrial tax which looks suspiciously like a selective employment tax. The anecdotes include other devices for revenue, such as cornering the market in grain, applying an import duty rigorously to overseas ambassadors, or charging a fee for the registration of slaves as an insurance policy against their running away.

One economic change which we can trace in the Hellenistic age is the increased production of articles somewhere between high-grade luxury goods and cheap material for the consumption of the poor. We can see this clearly in the pottery industry. Local coarse wares continue with little change of technique. The highest-quality Attic wares are produced (though with deteriorating design) throughout the third century. What is new is the mass production of pottery in imitation of silver and gold, which must have been neither very cheap nor very expensive, such as the so-called Megarian bowls. Something similar seems to have happened in the field of clothing, which remained for the most part a cottage industry. But we can trace increasing specialization, in Bolus Democriteus' treatise on dyeing, for example, and some scholars think that there was factory production in the capital cities. The Pergamene court encouraged specialized treatises on aspects of agriculture; the monarch might even contribute to the series himself.

There was of course a substructure of slavery everywhere except in Egypt (where the main slave-owners, apart from a few immigrants, were in Hellenized Alexandria). Business increased with the advent of the Romans; L. Aemilius Paullus in 167 B C enslaved 150,000 Epirotes, and under Rome the slave-market at Delos boasted a turnover of 10,000 slaves a day. But Rome did not introduce slavery, and the

31 White slip figurine of a slave being flogged, from Priene. It is thought to have been suspended on a string for children to whip

theme of the free man or woman kidnapped or taken into slavery as prisoner of war is too prominent in New Comedy for it to lack all basis in fact.

> You've caught it now: it's the will of the gods.
> Better put up with it cheerfully; it'll be easier for you.
>   I expect you were free at home.
> Well you're slaves now; it's horse sense to get used to it
> and to obey any orders; use your savvy to make your passage
>   easy.

(Plautus, The Prisoners)

The first book of *Economics* attributed to Aristotle is a work of his school (Philodemus thought its author was Theophrastus), written early in the Hellenistic age. The attitude to slavery must have been fairly typical of enlightened thought at this period. 'Of possessions the primary, most indispensable, best and most essential to our estate is the human being.' There are two kinds of slaves. Some can be entrusted with responsibility, some do manual work; the former will need careful training. All slaves should be rewarded for good work and punished for bad; the balance of work, punishment and food must be carefully held. They should be given occasional treats, but not allowed wine.

57

They should be able to work towards a goal of freedom, but the owner will be well advised to avoid purchasing too many slaves of the same tribe, and to acquire hostages by encouraging his slaves to produce children. It is modestly humane, but the last clause shows that there was in fact a war on. Even Stoic humanitarianism did not abolish slavery. Zeno might dream of an ideal commonwealth in which there were no family divisions, nation-states, racial differences, slave or free, but Chrysippus defined a slave as a 'permanent hired labourer', and in so doing no more condemned slavery than he condemned free labour. It is only with the Roman Stoics that we find any sense that slavery is unnatural, and they had no impulse to social change: slavery remained the standing contrast between 'the law of the nations' and 'the law of Nature'.

The economic health of the Hellenistic age is a matter of controversy among diagnosticians. This can be seen in the respective views of Kahrstedt and Rostovtzeff. Kahrstedt saw the third century as an age of enlightened humanity, and the Hellenistic age generally as a period of progressive economic advance. The development of capitalism with backing from the central government was reducing the dependence on slavery and encouraging free labour. The coming of Rome destroyed all that was being achieved and held European economy back for two thousand years. Rostovtzeff admitted that the Hellenistic rulers benefited the economy by opening up new lands and by an advanced technology not previously known in the East, but he blamed the ultimate failure of the Hellenistic powers not upon the intrusion of Rome, but upon internal factors, in particular the rigid control of centralized planning and the bureaucratic stagnation and opportunities for corruption that went with it. Both Kahrstedt and Rostovtzeff were really arguing *a priori* from their own attitudes to socialism, and were too facile in applying analogies from modern history. Each could find plenty of evidence to support a view he had initially not needed evidence to reach. The truth, as so often, is complex. Neither progress nor decline was constant. The second quarter of the third century was a period of prosperity, the third was one of recession, the fourth one of recovery. Similar fluctuations can be seen in the second century. Furthermore, in any single period we can discern a combination of success and failure. Merits and demerits, virtues and vices, enterprise and restriction, progress and decay, prosperity and adversity, walked side by side.

Men had already, in the imperfections of this world, begun to dream of a perfect society. Homer's Phaeacians offered one such idyll in which Nature conspires to create blessings; Hesiod's Golden Race another. Hitherto, as in Hippodamus or Phaleas or Plato or Aristotle, their dreams had been of a community whose bounds were strictly limited. A state of a hundred thousand people, says Aristotle, is as unthinkable as a ship a quarter of a mile long. Before Alexander all ideal communities were built on exclusiveness. All those after him are inclusive. What is more, Arnold Toynbee has argued that all Utopias except More's are attempts to peg back history and recapture that which has been lost or is in danger of being lost. The dictum is overstated; there are other exceptions besides More, as Edward Bellamy's *Looking Backward* may remind us. But in many cases it is illuminating. William Morris in *News from Nowhere* was attempting to return to a pre-industrial society. Plato in *The Republic* sought to retain the limited city-state. The dreams after Alexander do to some extent look back on what was lost when he died on 13 June 323 aged only thirty-two.

Zeno the Stoic was first. He wrote a book called *The Republic* while 'under the tail of the dog', i.e. under Cynic influence. It depicted a community of the wise, linked by the power of Love (Eros), free from sexual jealousy and family rivalries through the exercise of free love, having no temples, law-courts or gymnasia, no money and therefore no commerce. They would live in several cities but these cities would be part of a universal order; they would all be members of one flock and subject to one common law (there is a Greek pun here on 'law' and 'pasture'), regarding all men as their fellow-citizens. Plutarch, from whom the last evidence is taken, says that Alexander made real what Zeno dreamed.

Alexander's empire broke up among warring generals, and Cassander, Antipater's son, secured Macedon and Greece. Cassander was a ruthless politician, but also a man of some culture, whose importance here lies in his patronage of Euhemerus and his humouring of his brother Alexarchus. Euhemerus is best known as a rationalist who believed that the gods were historical characters who had subsequently been deified. But instead of presenting this in logical argument he chose to embody it in a sort of mythological novel, dealing with an island called the Sacred Isle or Panchaïa, which was said to lie some days' voyage out from the coast of Yemen, and including a description of the politics and geography of the island. In this we may notice six points.

First, Euhemerus is a Utopian in the strict sense of the word. He is perhaps the first theorist to assume ideal external conditions for his ideal political commonwealth. (This is brilliantly parodied by Lucian, who, however, sets his fantasy in the belly of a gigantic whale.) In Euhemerus' Utopia every prospect pleases, and not even man is vile. His predecessors had been concerned with problems of political administration in the Greece in which they lived. They sought to idealize the system of administration; they did not idealize those external and adventitious circumstances which are outside the control of man. They accepted the perfectibility of man, or at least of some men; they did not dream of the perfectibility of Nature. Euhemerus is responsible for turning political theory from its more obviously practical task of improving the existing polities to that of setting forth an ideal, of which man may dream, but which, because it denies that Nature has her ruthless side, he will not realize.

Secondly, Euhemerus' is a class society. There are three classes in Panchaïa, the upper comprising the priests and civil servants, the middle the farmers, and the lower the soldiers and herdsmen. It is important to notice that there is no economic or social privilege except for that of the priests, no industrialism and, above all, no slavery.

Thirdly, Euhemerus' state is limited in extent, but its citizenship is universal. The name Panchaïa and the name of the capital, Panara, both indicate universalism. In addition to the native Panchaïans there are Cretans representing the East and Oceanites representing the unknown peoples surrounding all. Panchaïa is a world-state in miniature.

Fourthly, Euhemerus, rationalist though he was, adopted some of the paraphernalia of Babylonian astronomy: Zeus came to Panchaïa from Babylon; the island's sacred stream is called 'Water of the Sun'; according to Pliny the City of the Sun stood near Panchaïa; one of the principal cities is called Asterusia; the name of the great mountain

32 The pursuit of the ideal commonwealth. Plato's Academy pictured on a mosaic from Pompeii

(later rationalized) is 'Heaven's throne'; Heaven or Uranus was an early inhabitant. This is all associated with the impartiality of the sun and heaven. The sun shines and the rain falls upon mankind without fear or favour. The eye of the sun sees all. The sun and sky are types of justice, a conception which it is vital to comprehend.

Fifthly, private property is practically non-existent and money completely abolished. The resources of the land are divided according to three principles. Everyone shall have a fair share proportionate to the actual resources. Those with special responsibilities shall receive more. There shall be adequate incentives for good work – a sort of Stakhanovite idea.

Sixthly, in government three different principles may be seen at work. There is monarchy; this is a reflection of the trend of the times, and the position of Alexander or Cassander; it is also a reflection of the more fundamental symbolism associated with the sun. Around Panara, however, the inhabitants make their own laws and elect their own ministers from any class; this egalitarianism is specially noteworthy. Finally, the priests, though without constitutional position, are the true experts and hold the effective power, being voluntarily consulted. This last inevitably leads us to think of the position of the church in the Middle Ages. There is also an interesting parallel, as elsewhere in Euhemerus, with Soviet Russia, where Stalin for a long period exercised the effective power without holding governmental office under the constitution.

Cassander also had an eccentric brother named Alexarchus, who founded a city called Uranopolis, the City of Heaven, on the peninsula which separates Mount Athos from the mainland. We know little enough about it, having only three obscure literary references and some coins, but what we know is fascinating and makes us wish for an excavation of the site to fill out some of the gaps in our knowledge. The name of the city is striking and unusual. It is recorded also in Pamphylia, but that town was perhaps a colony of Alexarchus' original foundation. In form the name is similar to Heliopolis (the City of the Sun) and Hierapolis. Alexarchus himself, we are told, identified himself with the Sun the all-ruler. He was a grammarian who invented a language for his city. Athenaeus quotes a letter of his and says, 'What this means I do not think even the Delphic Oracle could discern.' One thing it means is that he thought that he was founding a new sort of community, and perhaps a universal com-

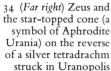

33 Silver coin of Uranopolis with the sun on the obverse and Urania on the reverse

34 (*Far right*) Zeus and the star-topped cone (a symbol of Aphrodite Urania) on the reverse of a silver tetradrachm struck in Uranopolis

munity; we may reflect on the way that protagonists of internationalism have devised Volapük, Esperanto, Ido, Interlingua, Interglossa and other tongues to break down the barriers of Babel. Further, this letter was written to the town of Cassandreia, and seems to begin not 'Alexarchus to the magistrates of Cassandreia, greeting', but 'Alexarchus to the chief men of the Brethren, rejoicing'. Brethren, though Cassandreia was separate, and a town of very mixed population. The boundaries of kin transcend the boundaries of government and race. The coins, which are very remarkable, show the same pattern of thought. They do not bear the name 'Uranopolitae', citizens of Uranopolis, but 'Uranidae', children of heaven, and they portray the sun, moon and stars, and the goddess Heavenly Aphrodite, goddess of heaven and of pure and universal love. All this points to one conclusion. In the mood of the times which followed Alexander, Alexarchus, echoing Euhemerus, was setting up a limited state which none the less expressed within its limited borders the brotherhood of man. Like most such limited community experiments it was doomed to failure and drops out of history; but, if this interpretation is right, it is an astonishing example of the new outlook.

Some fifty years or so later, shortly after 250 BC, an otherwise unknown author named Iambulus wrote a Utopian novel whose substance is preserved by Diodorus Siculus. There is a clear debt to Euhemerus and also to the Stoics. According to the story Iambulus is captured by Ethiopians and sent off on a four months' voyage to reach an island of blessedness. If he is successful, the Ethiopians will enjoy six hundred years of peace and prosperity. He eventually reaches the island, which is one of seven and has a perimeter of six hundred miles. He describes the people, and their life and constitution. They are called the 'Children of the Sun', and the islands are the Islands of the Sun.

Four features of his description call for our notice. First is the element of sheer Utopianism. The Children of the Sun display their equality through a physical equality. Their bodies are unusually large, their bones unusually pliant, their tongues and ears peculiarly formed (so that they can even carry on two conversations at the same time), their grasp impregnable, their lives of great length, their persons of exceptional beauty. The animals on the island are, as the author rightly says, incredible. There is a creature with four eyes and mouths, whose blood has magical healing properties; there is a bird which flies with babies on its back and may perhaps be the stork of European legend. The water from the hot springs never cools unless it is laced with cold. The sea is sweet to the taste, a miracle for which many bathers have yearned. The fruit trees bear all the year round, and many of the crops grow without attention. There is no disease. The people live in perfect happiness and unblemished bliss, a sort of community of Stoic sages, all joyfully accepting the law of destiny. After seven years the intruder is ejected, not for any offence, but because he has not attained to this perfection and might thus be a corrupting influence.

Secondly, equality and universalism are the rules of the community. This may be seen as inherent in the book's astrological tendencies. The islands are the Islands of the Sun, and there are seven of them, as the ancients recognized seven great heavenly bodies. The people are identical in form and stature; they hold their wives and children in common; there is no private property; they take it in turn to perform the duties of the community; at the age of 150 they commit euthanasial suicide and on death they are all alike entrusted to the power of the sea. This equality is important and characteristic.

Thirdly, as in all Hellenistic thinking, there is a high stress on education. We only have a very abbreviated account of this, but there is enough to see that it is directed to teaching about the fundamentals of religion and life, and to the formation of sterling character.

Fourthly, the general life of the people shows no slavery. They live the simple life. Work is honourable and all work is shared. Leisure is spent in mutual fellowship and in the praise of God. One is reminded of Epictetus many years later: the purpose of Man's life is to know God and to sing His praises.

These ideas affected a Stoic named Sphaerus, who was tutor to Cleomenes III, king of that Sparta which Toynbee has seen as the type of an 'arrested' civilization. We have already seen something of Cleomenes' revolution. It involved an equitable redistribution of economic resources. More, Cleomenes admitted resident aliens to citizenship, and issued a remarkable coinage in which his own head appeared within a type of Apollo, the sun-god (at least in one aspect); we are impelled to think back to Alexarchus. The pattern is there: equality, universality and the rule of the sun.

We move on another century. The dominant power in the Mediterranean is now Rome. Rome was governed by a narrow and exclusive senatorial aristocracy who had been forced across the centuries to concede theoretical equality to the commons but abrogated no more practical supremacy than men have to women in British politics. Further, economic domination by the aristocracy and the upper middle class had increased. The aristocrats were forbidden to trade by the *lex Claudia* of 218. So instead they bought up huge estates including common land.

> 'Tis bad enough in man or woman
> To steal a goose from off a common.
> But surely he's without excuse
> Who steals the common from the goose.

Into this situation came Tiberius Gracchus. His mother and sister-in-law were Scipios; his father-in-law, Appius Claudius Pulcher, the doyen of the senate, gave respectability to his cause. He was brought up by a Greek tutor named Blossius, a Stoic, and a man who knew his Iambulus. This is not the place to enter into detail about the history of the Gracchi; it is complex and controversial. In Cleomenes Iambulus' idealism was overlaid with ambitious nationalism, in the Gracchi with Roman aristocratic traditionalism. But it was there. Tiberius proposed measures to relieve economic distress with basic units of about twenty acres taken from the illegitimately inflated estates. The money to capitalize the farmers was to come from a convenient bequest from the eccentric King Attalus of Pergamum. Tiberius defied the senate and used illegal means to push his measures through. He was murdered, but his measures held and gave some

35 Silver *denarius* of the late Republic commemorating Tiberius Gracchus

75,000 more people economic security. Ten years later his brother Gaius tried again. His measures included food subsidies, new land settlements, and an attempt to extend the Roman citizenship at least within Italy. He, too, was put to death under martial law. Much modified, we see the same pattern recurring – social justice, the attack on the aristocracy in the name of political and social equity, and the extension of citizenship.

On Tiberius' death Blossius was tried for high treason, but acquitted. He left Rome, however, for Pergamum. Attalus III, as we have seen, had died and left a will bequeathing his possessions to the people of Rome. The will is certain, for the evidence of the historians is confirmed by epigraphic evidence; but its details are obscure. Evidently there was a situation of social unrest. In the interim the citizens of Pergamum conferred citizenship on classes of resident aliens, even raising some slaves to the same status. Then came Blossius and set himself by the side of one Aristonicus, pretender to the throne. We know next to nothing of Aristonicus, but we can discern three motives which drove him on – personal ambition, nationalist resentment against the bequest to Rome, and social reform and idealism. His movement began among the serfs on the large estates and spread among the semi-independent population of the hinterland. For the moment it seemed, and was, formidable. They proposed to form a new city, and its name was to be – the City of the Sun. In the East there was a long-standing connection between the sun, whose eye looks impartially on all things, and justice. The thought had a natural appeal for many Asiatics. Some modern interpreters think that this was all. But Blossius' presence suggests another factor in the City of the Sun. It was to be Iambulus' Utopia realized. Of course it failed; Roman military might and resilience in defeat were too great.

Aristonicus was captured and died in prison in Rome. But one would be glad to know more about this gallant and ill-fated experiment in practical idealism. Centuries later Tommaso Campanella, who had himself essayed the reformation of Calabria as a universal republic, called his Utopian vision the City of the Sun.

On another hundred years, and the mastery of Rome is now unquestioned. But a century of civil war has made men despair. Left wing has fought right, and each side in power has massacred the other; the Italians have revolted against Rome; slaves have risen against their masters and gladiators against their overlords; Caesar and Pompey have fought for the mastery of the Roman world, and Caesar in his turn has been murdered; so more civil war and more proscriptions, with Cicero one of the first to go. And now an uneasy truce, with Octavian, the future Augustus, master of Italy, and Antony overlord of the East, and flirting with Cleopatra in Alexandria. The consul is one Pollio, Antony's man and a moderate. The year is 40 B C. Vergil, Epicurean and pacifistic, a young poet with little except juvenilia behind him, wrote a poem which we call the 'Messianic Eclogue'. A child is to be born, with whom the maiden Justice will descend to earth, and the age of Saturn, the golden age, will come anew; this is somehow Pollio's doing and will start in Pollio's consulship. The child will rule a world brought to peace by his father's prowess. The earth will bring forth untended, the herds will not fear the lion, and sheep will wander over the pastures with their fleeces ready dyed (though here we must agree with T. E. Page that the step from the sublime to the ridiculous is a small one, and Vergil has misjudged it). Be gracious to the Baby's birth, immaculate goddess of childbirth and light; your Apollo rules at last: *casta fave Lucina, tuus iam regnat Apollo!* Pollio had organized a marriage between Antony and Octavian's sister Octavia. The poem was written for the prospective child of that marriage. But it is the ingredients which concern us here – a new reign of peace and prosperity for all; Justice descending from heaven; Nature conspiring as in the dreams of Euhemerus or Iambulus; and the child growing to kingship under the reign of Apollo, the sun-god. The ingredients are the same; the essential pattern identical.

Antony, a simple soldier who liked his wenches, now had the experience, unfamiliar to him, of being married to a thoroughly good woman. For two years or so it lasted. They wintered in Greece, and Antony took an interest in education and attended the lectures of the philosophers. But it could not go on. Three things conspired to break it. There was from the wedding no son, only a daughter. Antony became convinced that ultimately he could not co-operate with Octavian's insatiable ambition. The memory of Cleopatra stirred in his blood, and by the end of 37 BC he had packed Octavia back to Italy, met Cleopatra and married her. We must not underestimate Cleopatra. The woman who could impress Cicero by her knowledge of philosophy, who had the business acumen and technical knowledge to run a wool-mill, whom it was enough for generations of Egyptians to call 'the queen', whom a seventh-century Coptic bishop praised as 'the most illustrious and wise among women', 'great in herself and in her achievements and in courage and in strength' – she is not to be dismissed as if she were some Hollywood cutie with the right vital statistics. 'Rome', wrote Tarn, 'who had never condescended to fear any nation or people, did in her time fear two human beings; one was Hannibal, and the other was a woman'; and when Vergil in his epic of Rome's greatness sought for one figure in which to sum up the dangers which Rome had faced, he took the figure of a woman, Dido. Cleopatra aspired to be mistress of the world. She had a vision, a prophecy. She would cast down Rome from heaven to earth, then raise her from earth to heaven, inaugurate a golden age for Asia and Europe alike, and end feud, war and bloodshed.

> Tranquil peace shall journey to the land of Asia.
> Europe shall then be blessed, the atmosphere be fruitful,
> lasting, sturdy, free from storm or hail,
> bearing all creatures of the world, winged and earthbound.
> Blessed above all the man or woman who shall see that day. . . .
> For from the starry sky, in its fullness the rule of law
> and righteousness will descend upon man, and with it
> the saving grace of concord, cherished beyond all else by mortals,
> love, trust, friendship with the stranger. Far from men
> poverty will flee, compulsion will flee,
> and lawlessness, carping, envy, anger, folly,
> murder and deadly strife and bitter conflict,
> robbery by night and every evil – in those days.

(*Oracula Sibyllina* 3, 367–80: ll. 371–2 defective; ll. 377–8 transposed)

These are the same ingredients again, with Heaven brooding over all, Nature co-operating supernaturally, the nations mixed as in a loving-cup, and the kingdom of peace and justice made reality. Cleopatra renamed the eldest boy she bore to Antony Alexander Helios – 'Alexander the Sun'.

Perhaps it was propaganda only. At least it was worth putting out as propaganda. And we must not forget that we see Cleopatra through the eyes of her enemies. The ruthless military realism of Octavian conquered. Antony committed suicide and died in his lover's arms. She was captured by a ruse and encouraged to take the same way out. With the rule of the sun still in her mind she chose the asp, which ministered to the sun-god and deified those whom it struck. The Roman soldiers burst in on the scene. 'Is this well done, Charmian?', said one of them to the last dying handmaid. 'Yes,' she replied proudly. 'It is well done.'

On another hundred years to Nero. Nero in this pattern? *Que fait-il dans cette galère?* But yes. Rome was now an unregenerate monarchy. It had known the ruthless and egotistical genius of Augustus, the morose tactlessness of Tiberius and the treachery of his chief minister, the brutal megalomania of Caligula and the harmless eccentricities of the undignified Claudius, whose wisdom in general government was somewhat overlaid by his ludicrous private life and the behaviour of his upstart ministers. Now came this brilliant, apparently amiable boy, with marked artistic sensibilities, under the tutelage of the most sententious moral philosopher of the day. Surely the future was brightening.

The days of Saturn, the maiden Justice have returned;
our age has found safety in return to the ways of old.
The harvester stores his whole crop, hopeful, carefree;
the wine-god is mature and slow; the herds browse unattended;
the harvest is not with the sword; towns do not block their walls
in preparation for ominous war; no woman, dangerous
in motherhood, brings an enemy to birth. Unarmed our young
    men
dig the fields, and the lad trained to the plough's slow movement
gapes at the sword which hangs in his father's house. . . .
Now the earth bears fresh crops in plenty untilled.
Now the ships are secure, the waves lay anger and penance aside.

Tigers gnaw the bit. Lions put on the harsh yoke.
Be gracious, immaculate goddess of childbirth and light; your
    Apollo reigns at last.
    Casta fave Lucina, tuus iam regnat Apollo!

So the Einsiedeln Eclogue, and a coin with the head of Nero on the obverse and on the reverse a coiled snake with corn and poppyhead, emblems of fertility, shows Nero as the *Agathos Daimon*, the good genius of the new age.

Yet there was ill-omen in the air as well. Seneca greeted the new reign with a treatise, *On Clemency*. Nero is to look from the height on which he stands at ordinary, quarrelsome mankind, and to say to himself: 'I have been selected to perform on earth the office of the Gods, I am lord of life, death, and destiny. But I bear the sword of severity sheathed, and wear instead the breastplate of Clemency.' The very commendation of clemency is a reminder of how absolute was the power that wielded it. For all his occasional impulsive generosity, it is impossible to whitewash Nero. Temperament and affectation passed into cruelty and debauchery. To the Romans he was a tyrant and a mountebank, to the Christians Antichrist. One revolt was checked with carnage. The next succeeded, and Nero died with the words, 'What an artist the world is losing in me!' Only in Greece was he mourned. They had flattered his artistry: he had said that the Greeks alone knew how to be an audience, and proposed to rename the Peloponnesus Neronesus. For years the Greeks dreamed of Nero Redivivus, who would come again and with his second advent inaugurate the age of gold.

Expectation was in the air in Judaea, too. But their hope could not lie in a Nero or a child of Antony and Octavia. The Hellenistic age was for the Jews a period of apocalyptic vision, of the coming of the Day of the Lord, the Kingdom or Kingship of God, established in some traditions by God's anointed Messiah, who is in 1 Enoch called the Son of Man. Like other Hellenistic visions this was not a mere escapist dream: it was linked to history, and associated in the Book of Daniel with the rebellion against the idolatry imposed by Antiochus Epiphanes, and by later leaders and writers with the revolt against Rome.

In Nero's reign for the first time we find prominent in Rome a new movement. It was a revolutionary movement, which was why the

Romans hated it. It spread among the slaves and the poor artisans and the city mob, the discontented and disaffected. It loved an ancient poem which prophesied the coming of the golden age with the birth of a child, an age when the wolf shall dwell with the lamb and the leopard with the kid, and there shall be no hurt or destruction. It sang a revolutionary song, 'He has put down the mighty from their seats and has exalted the humble and meek; he has filled the hungry with good things and the rich he has sent empty away.' It brought peace and justice by an actual and practical refusal to use weapons of war and by sharing of possessions and resources. It followed a Master who declared that the impartiality of its adherents was to be that of the sun or rain, the old motif of the all-covering heaven and its all-seeing eye. It acknowledged no barriers of race or nationality, class, or sex; Jew or Gentile, bond or free, man or woman – here they were all one. It proclaimed one King and His Kingdom made real wherever his authority was plain in the life of individual or community. When after many years an emperor was found to profess the faith of Christianity Lactantius addressed him in words which have their clear links with the pattern we have been examining: 'I begin my work under the auspices of your name, Constantine, Emperor Supreme, first of Roman rulers to renounce error, first to know and honour the majesty of the one true God. For when that happiest of days shone on the earth in which Almighty God raised you to the blessed height of empire, you gave a splendid omen that your government would be wholesome and desirable for all your subjects by restoring routed and banished Justice and thus expiating the fearful crime of other men. For this deed God shall give you happiness, virtue and length of days, that loyal to this same Justice which guided you in your youth, you may in old age hold fast the tiller of the state, and receiving the great charge from your father, transmit to your children the custody of the Roman name.' These words were more than a trifle optimistic. Military realism and middle-class respectability seized hold of that movement, too, and corrupted it. The vision of Utopia is ever before us, never ours.

36 The archetypal
philosopher. Detail
of a first-century
BC wall-painting
from Boscoreale,
near Pompeii

V WITHDRAWAL

Gilbert Murray in a famous phrase which he derived from J. B. Bury characterized the Hellenistic age by 'the failure of nerve'. The Olympian gods had failed to save; there was no certainty, no security there. At the same time individuals felt themselves no longer masters of their own fate and captains of their own soul. Life was uncertain. What power held the wheel?

Perhaps Fortune, Chance, *Tyche*. Demetrius of Phalerum, Aristotelian and politician, began the succession of treatises on Fortune. In reflecting on Macedon's rise and Alexander's career he wrote: 'No need to look back endlessly through time, generation after generation; the last fifty years show the violence of Fortune. . . . Fortune is not affected by the way we live; she transforms everything against all expectation; she reveals her power in the unexpected. At this moment I suspect that in establishing the Macedonians in the former glory of the Persians she is demonstrating that they have those blessings on loan only, till she changes her mind about them.' This was the mood of the times. Polybius himself succumbed to it. However much he might insist on a more rational theory of causality, he also introduced Chance as a factor in history. It has been suggested that this represents a change of attitude; but both are embedded alike in the earlier and later parts of his history. Even Theophrastus could say, 'Fortune, not counsel, guides human affairs'. So a character in Menander, always an index of the times, says:

> Stop blathering about will. Human will
> adds up to nothing. Fortune's will –
> call it divine spirit or intelligent will –
> it is that pilots the universe, steers
> and saves. Mortal forethought is gas
> and gaiters. Listen to me. You won't regret it.
> All we will, all we say, all we do
> is Fortune; we simply add our signatures. . . .

Fortune pilots the universe. She is the goddess
solely entitled to the names intelligence and forethought,
unless we are foolish enough to love empty words.

Here is another comic dramatist, Diphilus:

Fortune's like a barmaid mixing us a drink,
putting in one measure of good liquor and adding three of bad.

Here, too, is a fragment of a lyric invocation:

Fortune, for men
the alpha and the omega, throned in wisdom's chair,
dispensing glory to human action,
blessings more than curses – such the grace
that gleams about your golden wings.
What your balance grants is a lasting blessing.
You have found a way for the helpless in distress.
You have shined your light in the darkness, goddess of grace.

The mood lasts long: it is found as late as the third century AD:

Many-hued, multiformed, wingfooted,
Man's almighty companion – Fortune.
How should we display your power . . . ?
Your eye lights on all that is proud and exalted;
you throw a cloud and darkness round and dash it to the ground.
Often you raise up high on your wings
the humble and low, mighty spirit.
Should we call you dark Clotho,
or swift-dooming Compulsion,
or Iris, the gods' swift messenger?
The beginning and end of all are in your hands.

A passage from the elder Pliny expresses the mood well: it is doubtless
derived from some Hellenistic source: 'Throughout the world
everywhere at every moment by every voice Fortune and none but
she is invoked by name: she is the one defendant, the one in the dock,
the one topic, the one heroine, the one responsible, honoured and
reproached at once. She is fickle, in the eyes of many blind, erratic,
unreliable, changeful, friend of the worthless. To her is debited all our
expenditure, to her is credited all our income; she without other

37 An unusual relief showing *Agathe Tyche* as the wife of Zeus

support occupies both pages of the human balance-sheet. We are so dependent on Chance that Chance proves God uncertain and takes his place.' So at Elis Pausanias saw a sanctuary of *Tyche* with a colossal cult statue; in Thebes he saw a cult statue of her with the infant Wealth in her arms; and in the remarkable relief at Copenhagen Good Fortune, *Agathe Tyche*, is the wife of Zeus the Fulfiller, God of Friendship. Good Fortune was regularly invoked, even in consulting the oracle of Zeus at Dodona. Epitaphs, though more hostile, tell the same story. Already in the fourth century Fortune is described as jealous of virtue. She is irrational. The grave inscription of a certain Phileremus reveals that the dead man's friends saw her as a tyrant whose whim called him away from life.

If not Fortune then perhaps the heavenly bodies were responsible for life's uncertainties. Astrology was strong and of long standing in Mesopotamia. An age uncertain of itself and newly in touch with the East naturally turned that way. The gods were as remote as the kings; the heavenly bodies were at least visible, like governors of garrisons. Perhaps they were the gods.

Seven wandering stars wheel their way through the gate
of Olympus, with mingled among them ageless Time –
the Moon, light of the darkness; stern Kronos; the adorable Sun;
the queen of Paphos, escort of brides; fierce Ares; winged Hermes;
Zeus, best, noblest of all, source of all nature.
They have received by lot articulate man. Among us are
the Moon, Zeus, Ares, the Paphian, Kronos, the Sun, Hermes.
So it is our lot to receive from the holy air above
sorrow, laughter, anger, life, reason, sleep, desire.
Kronos brings tears, Zeus gives us birth, Hermes offers understanding,
Ares sends anger, the Moon sends sleep, Aphrodite sends desire,
yes, and we derive laughter from the Sun: the Sun makes all
nature smile,
Man's mind, and the infinite universe.

(Anon. in Stobaeus, Eclogae 1)

The general belief is given by Diodorus, drawing on (and blurring)
earlier sources. He speaks with some admiration of the long traditions,
careful observations and organized system of the Chaldaeans. They
call the planets 'Interpreters' because they interpret the will of the
gods to mankind. Their risings, settings and colour are signs of what
is to come, meteorological phenomena and natural disasters. Under
the 7 Interpreters are 30 divine Counsellors, 15 above and 15 below
the earth; above them are 12 Overlords, each having his own month
and his own sign of the zodiac. The planets affect human beings at
their birth, and the Chaldaeans were able to predict the success of
Alexander, Antigonus and Seleucus as well as the destinies of lesser
folk. The deterministic Stoics fostered these superstitions: Poseidonius
was especially vulnerable. But not only the Stoics. Theophrastus, if
we can trust Proclus, regarded the Chaldaean prophecies as the most
astonishing feature of his day. In less intellectual circles belief was
widespread. The astrological deities are the powers, rulers, lords,
thrones, principalities, powers of the height and depth which Paul is
always assuring his readers are subject to Christ.

Epicurus stood apart from these things. But he stood apart from
much else too, and in this equally represents the mood of the times.
He was an Athenian, born about 341 BC and brought up in Samos. He
returned to Athens briefly in 323, but was driven out by other

philosophers, and spent some time in Colophon and Mytilene. In 306 he was able to return, and bought a house with a large garden, off the Piraeus road. Here he built up a fellowship of friends and disciples in which there were no barriers of class, sex or age. Here, far from the madding crowd's ignoble strife, they kept the noiseless tenor of their way. For Epicurus, living in an age when the community had ceased to count, held that the object of life could only be pleasure; in this (though he acknowledged no debt) he followed the Cyrenaics. But he did not interpret pleasure crudely; he saw, and said, that our impulse to pleasure starts with the body, with food and sex, but was maligned as if he had said that it finished there. In fact he held to the hedonistic calculus: confronted with a choice of action we should choose that which offers the largest excess of pleasure over pain, or the smallest excess of pain over pleasure. Epicurus therefore espoused the simple life, because ultimately it contains more pleasure: if you habitually eat dry bread, a piece of cheese gives you a pleasure which the gourmand never knows. He also claimed that morality was a means to pleasure; it was impossible to live a pleasant life without living a wise, just and honest life. In fact Epicurus' key word is not pleasure but *ataraxia*, freedom from disturbance. The main disturbers of our peace are fears and desires – fear of death, pain, gods, and desires which are neither natural nor necessary. His prescription of salvation was the Fourfold Cure, in Greek twelve words:

> God is not an object of fear.
> Death is not an object of sensation.
> Good can be easily attained.
> That which we fear can be easily endured.

A simple analysis shows that desires are either natural and necessary (such as the desire for food), natural and unnecessary (such as the desire for interesting food), or unnatural and unnecessary (such as the desire for power, fame or riches). The third we should eliminate. 'Live out of the public eye,' said Epicurus in a famous phrase, and Seneca rightly pointed a difference when he said that according to Zeno the wise man will engage in public life unless something prevents him, according to Epicurus the wise man will not engage in public life unless something compels him. Pain cannot be eliminated, and Epicurus actually said that the wise man will be happy even on the rack. But we know one thing of pain: if it is long, it is light; if it is

38 Bust of Epicurus   39 Zeno the Stoic

sharp, it is short. For the rest the answer to fear is knowledge, science, and the whole impressive structure of Epicurean science is an answer to fear.

The first step towards truth is clear thinking, and the first part of Epicurus' philosophy is his 'canonic' or rules of thought. Our mind is presented with four types of evidence: feeling, sense-experience, preconception and intuitive reflection. Feeling is the experience of pleasure and pain, and Epicurus held that it gave reliable knowledge of the cause of the pleasure or pain; in this he differed from Aristippus. So, too, sense-experience gives certain knowledge of the object which has caused the experience, and all sense-impressions are alike true; error enters when we try to interpret our experiences. A preconception is not to be understood in an absolute sense: it is a recollection of an external object which has been apprehended more than once, a general notion stored in the mind; it is this that enables us to make judgments which go beyond our immediate experience. Intuitive reflection enables us to take a comprehensive view and grasp the general system of the universe.

The second part of Epicurus' philosophy is his physics, and we have his own summary treatment of it in his letter to his disciple Herodotus. Nothing exists except atoms and void; this, though again he disowned his debt, he owed to Democritus and Nausiphanes. But whereas in the earlier atomists the atoms were moving at random and by their accidental collisions set up a vortex, Epicurus, aware of the effects of gravity, attributed to the atoms a downward motion. Further, he knew that objects of different mass falling in a vacuum fall with identical velocity. It follows that within the mechanistic system the atoms will never collide and come together to form a world. But they have formed a world. We must therefore postulate in the atoms a power of swerving from their course which is not the determined product of scientific law. It is important to see that Epicurus is presenting a physical solution to a problem in physics; this done, he equally saw it as the point at which free will may enter a mechanistic universe. 'It is better to accept the fables about the gods than to be a slave to the predestination of the physical scientists.' Just so did J.S. Compton in the twentieth century use Heisenberg's Uncertainty Principle for the same end.

Here, as Augustine saw, Epicurus broke with Democritus. Cicero and Seneca are sarcastic about the swerve – 'a schoolboy's invention' – but it was in fact a shrewd scientific hypothesis. The number of atoms is infinite, and the variety of their shapes uncountably large; the void is infinite in extent. It follows that there exists an infinite number of worlds. Because nothing exists except atoms and void, everything that exists is composed of atoms and every event is to be explained in terms of the movement or contact of atoms. In these terms, for example, we must explain sense-perception. In sight a minute film of atoms is detached from the object seen and impinges upon the perceiving eye; we may compare the photons of the modern physicist. The qualities which we apprehend with the senses, except for shape, size and weight, do not belong to the atoms themselves. We can now see how Epicurus' physics conduces to peace of mind. In the first place, it goes far to eliminate fear of the unknown. In the second place, natural phenomena, such as thunder and lightning, which the superstitious interpret as the anger of the gods, are explained in physical terms. In the third place, the soul, the inner personality, being atomic in structure (or it could not exist), is subject to dissolution, and we need have no fear of punishment after death. 'Death is nothing to us; for that which has suffered dissolution has no feeling; and that which has no feeling is nothing to us.'

Epicurus' ethics, the third and culminating part of his philosophy, we have already examined. They are conveniently summarized in a letter to Menoeceus. This begins with the importance of the search for wisdom. Then Epicurus expounds his philosophy. First, gods exist; he defends this in terms of our vision of them in dreams (which must have a physical origin), and because we have a preconception of them. They enjoy eternal bliss; from other sources we know that he regarded them as compounded of very fine atoms, and located in the *metakosmia* or *intermundia*, the areas between the worlds, so that they would not be involved in the dissolution of the worlds. A curious doctrine of balance suggested that there must be immortal beings to balance the mortal. Epicurus is bitter about popular superstition. 'Real blasphemy is not eliminating the gods of the masses but attributing to the gods a picture of them held by the masses.' The gods are not concerned with us. But effluxes emanating from them can help the man who is rightly attuned to receive them.

Death is nothing. The wise man does not take offence at life or fear death. In life, the future is neither wholly in our control nor wholly outside our control; dogmatic hope and despair are alike out of place. There follows a sermon on the elimination of desire, and the pursuit of a pleasure which does not mean sensuality, but freedom of the body from pain and the soul from disturbance, a pleasure which is inseparable from right living. Epicurus did not, however, believe in absolute justice, and when asked why a man should not behave in an anti-social manner, could only answer, 'Because you can never be certain that you won't be found out.' Justice is in fact a compact of expediency, and with glorious self-contradiction Epicurus makes fear its sanction.

To this general picture we may add two points. The first is that Epicurus gave an account of the emergence of civilization which in its broad outlines would be acceptable to modern anthropology. The life of man was originally, as Thomas Hobbes put it, 'solitary, poor, nasty, brutish, and short', till necessity proved the mother of invention, language was developed from natural animal cries, and men banded together for mutual convenience and security. The other point is the exaltation of friendship. Of course Epicurus was bound to base his theory of friendship on expediency. His practice transcended that, however, as an attractive fragment of a letter to a little girl shows. Some of his words on friendship have a rare warmth: 'Friendship dances round the world, calling to us all to awaken to the joys of a happy life.'

He was a remarkable man. Other schools changed their tenets almost beyond recognition; it is sometimes hard to see Carneades as being in the stream from Plato, or Marcus Aurelius in the stream from Zeno. But Lucretius and Diogenes of Oenoanda do not add or subtract much from the original teaching of Epicurus. His birthday continued to be celebrated by his disciples. Lucretius pays tribute to him again and again, hailing him as a god who called our lives out of darkness and placed them in the light. Faith he lacked, but he had charity.

Epicurus was a dogmatist who challenged the dogmas of others. Contemporary with him was an intellectual movement which challenged all dogma. Scepticism as a systematic philosophy went back to Pyrrho, who was with Alexander on his expedition, and returned to his native city of Elis to preach for forty years the doctrine of intellectual uncertainty. 'Truth is unknowable.' 'There is no argument which cannot be refuted.' 'The senses are deceivers.' 'This is as good as that.' Peace of mind comes from recognition of our limitations. Pyrrho influenced the biting pen of Timon, best known for his *Silloi* or *Squint-Eyed Poems*, in which he left no one unstung: Zeno the Stoic appeared as 'that greedy old Semitic woman', and Socrates is 'a wizard who enchanted Greece'. More surprisingly the attitude passed to Plato's successors in the Academy. Arcesilaus held that absolute truth was beyond the human intellect. The wise man must therefore suspend judgment, though he may take probability as his guide. In this philosophy he was backed in the following century by Carneades (*c.* 215–129), the most acute mind of Greece between Aristotle and Plotinus. We cannot attain knowledge of the simplest things. The colours on a pigeon's neck change in the light; a square tower looks round in the distance; a painter can delude us into thinking his painting is three-dimensional; we cannot tell whether we are moving past a scene or it is moving past us. Sense-perception is unreliable. But so are fundamental assumptions. God, for example, cannot be both infinite and endowed with definite characteristics. Nor can God possess any virtue, for all virtues consist in overcoming some imperfection. These, and many other arguments, were directed against Stoic dogmatism. They were equally valid against Platonic dogmatism, and the change from dogmatism to scepticism is an index of the movement of history between Plato and Carneades.

The mood of withdrawal is seen in the cultivation of pastoral poetry – an escape to an idyllic world of nymphs and shepherds, sunlight and summer, grazing goats and pan pipes. The great exponent of this type of poetry was Theocritus, who came to Alexandria after a childhood in Sicily and studies on the island of Cos, and was writing in the second quarter of the third century. In the first of all Theocritus' poems Thyrsis meets a goatherd and sings for him *The Dirge of Daphnis*:

> Begin my country song, dear Muses, begin.
> I am Thyrsis from Etna, this is Thyrsis' lovely voice.
> Where were you, Nymphs, where were you, when Daphnis
> pined away . . . ?
> Begin my country song, dear Muses, begin.

In other poems we meet Daphnis, and hear him competing with other herdsmen in song. It is all very charming, and very artificial. The traditions of Theocritus were carried on by Bion and Moschus, of whom the former survives for us mainly in fragments:

> Let Love summon the Muses! Let the Muses escort Love!
> Let the Muses ever give me song at my desire,
> mellifluous song; there is no more welcome cure.

40, 41 Carneades of Cyrene, founder and director of the 'Third Academy'. (*Right*) Silver dish with a pastoral scene and a shepherd thought to represent Theocritus

42 Gold diadem found at Canosa in south-east Italy. The opulent intricacy of the craftsmanship and the artificiality of the subject offer a telling symbol of the Hellenistic spirit

His *Lament for Adonis* has some power, though not as much as Moschus' *Lament for Bion*:

> Begin a song of grief, Muses of Sicily, begin.
> Ah! when the mallows or the green parsley
> or the curling proliferating anise wither in the garden,
> they come to life again and spring up for another year.
> But we humans, big and strong, for all our wisdom,
> when once we are dead, lie heedless in the hollow earth
> and sleep sound and long a sleep without end or waking.

Mostly this is escapist literature, dreaming of an ideal world free from the hurly-burly of city and court. It remains escapist when Vergil or Spenser takes it up.

Theocritus finds a parallel in some highly mannerist jewellery from Magna Graecia. An astonishing diadem from a tomb at Canosa consists of two strips of gold hinged together and covered with exquisite ornamentation in the form of artificial flowers and leaves formed of gold, enamel and precious stones. Even the less elaborate wreaths where the leaves are simulated in gold breathe the same spirit. This is the mood in which a refined, artificial culture looked at country life, refined it and made it artificial.

The great prophet of withdrawal belonged to an older generation. This was Diogenes, nicknamed 'the Dog'. His followers were called 'Dog-philosophers' or 'Cynics', a term which has since changed its meaning. From about 340 to 320 Diogenes was active as an itinerant preacher, without citizenship, without home, without possessions, defying convention, inuring himself to hardship by lying in the winter snow embracing a marble statue, or rolling in the scorching sand

83

beneath the blazing summer sun. Like Housman's Terence, he trained for ill and not for good. This tells us something about Diogenes and those who came after him; they expected ill. It also tells us something about the attitudes of the age. Plato, anecdotally, described him as 'Socrates gone mad': he might have taken it as a compliment.

We can see the Cynics of the mid-third century through the eyes of Leonidas of Tarentum, one of the earliest and most attractive of the Hellenistic epigrammatists. On the one hand he is prepared to play with the popular impression of the Cynic:

> Wallet and hard old goatskin,
> flask and staff for his tread,
> empty purse of dogskin,
> hat for his blasphemous head,
> these are the spoils that Famine
> won from Sochares – dead.

But he honoured Diogenes himself:

> Sad servant of death, crossing these waters
>   of Acheron in your dark ferry,
> though your boat is overloaded with the dead,
>   take me on board, the Dog Diogenes.
> My luggage is a wallet and flask and an old
>   cloak, and a penny to buy a ticket.
> I come, bringing to Death all that I owned
>   in life, leaving nothing beneath the sun.

43 A stylized Flavian representation of Diogenes confronting the young Alexander from his tub

44 An itinerant Cynic equipped for the road

Many of his other epigrams show the theme of the emptiness of life:

Measureless time or ever your years, O man, were reckoned;
   measureless time shall run over you in the ground.
And your life between is – what? The flick of a flying second,
   a flash, a point – or less – if a lesser thing can be found. . . .
Ask, O man, what your strength is worth each day that's breaking.
   Rest content with a little; simplicity be your law;
always recall as long as you dwell among the waking
   how you are made and fitted together from stalks of straw.
                              (tr. E. Bevan, altered)

The most attractive of the Cynics was Crates, a rich man who gave away his fortune in order to follow the way of life indicated by Diogenes; the comparison with Francis of Assisi has often been made and is apt. But Crates had another woman in his life besides Poverty. This was Hipparchia, and their marriage was a deep and lasting love match of a kind rare in the ancient world, since it was based upon an affinity of noble minds, and they shared their lives, side by side, in a way to which ancient Greece was unaccustomed. The service which men like Crates did to education is seen in the experience of Hipparchia's brother Metrocles, who found studying under Theophrastus or Xenocrates so expensive as quickly to run through a generous allowance, whereas under Crates he was taught to live simply, unextravagantly, and with far more contentment.

As with Socrates, it is what Crates was rather than what he taught that matters. He attacked hedonism with wit and urbanity. There is some indication that he demanded simple living rather than the complete renunciation of all possessions; he did not, like other Cynics, resort to that mendicancy which is the weakness of the extreme Cynic position, since it seeks one's own salvation at the expense of others. He was of course a pacifist; he could see too clearly the futility of war. He wrote a poem about an imaginary country called 'Walletchia' (named from the wallet or scrip which the Cynics carried):

There is a country Walletchia in a wine-dark sea of delusion,
beautiful, fruitful, and pretty squalid, with no possessions.
Never a fool and never a sponger and never a lecher
taking delight in a prostitute's body sails to that country.
But it produces figs, garlic and loaves of bread, thyme in its
   strength.

85

Then thus men don't declare war on each other in search of these
  prizes,
don't take up arms for the motive of profit or even for glory.

Some lines from one of his tragedies sum up his beliefs:

> My country has no single tower, no single roof.
> Its citadel belongs to all the world; its home
> stands ready for us to occupy.

They called him 'the Door-Opener' from his practice of entering
houses uninvited to preach to the inhabitants.

Bion of Borysthenes was influenced by Crates – Horace said he
was a man of 'black salt', meaning caustic wit – and something of what
he stood for can be seen in sayings of his follower Teles recorded by
John Stobaeus. Get rid of your possessions: they are only on deposit.
Find your food in the roads and rivers. One cloak will serve you;
double your summer cloak and you have a winter cloak. Nation,
tribe, the extended family – these are nothing. What do you lose in
exile? Anxiety about dependents! Your friends may die, even your
children: that's no reason for killing yourself. 'Fortune is like a
dramatist who designs a number of parts – the shipwrecked man, the
poor man, the exile, the king, the beggar. What the good man has to
do is to play well any part for which Fortune casts him.' 'That was a
splendid saying of the skipper, "All right, Poseidon, but she's on
course?" So a good man may say to Fortune "All right, but you're
sinking a man not a coward."' Pessimistic, individualistic, escapist
perhaps, but not ignoble.

What this is about is *autarky*, self-sufficiency. The old certainties
were gone. The man in the street was groping for something new,
Fortune or the Stars. The thinking man looked for his certainty in
himself. All the philosophies of the age exalt autarky. But ultimately
to pursue autarky is to cut yourself off from others. So Epicureans and
Cynics withdrew from society. Stoics did not, but they accounted
pity a vice, a sickness of the soul, a weakness of the tearful eye. So even
did the Neo-Platonists. For to pity another's misfortune is to lay your
peace of mind on the altar of circumstance: it is to sacrifice autarky.
Ultimately all these philosophies involved a withdrawal; they were
escapist.

The Hellenistic age was a restless age. People – or at least the people who made public history – were constantly searching. Alexander's *pothos*, his continual yearning for something not yet attained, infected the centuries which followed. Think of the relentless activity of Demetrius the Besieger. The years from 307 saw him in Ephesus, across the Aegean in Athens, defeating Ptolemy off the coast of Cyprus, coasting Egypt, besieging Rhodes, back to Athens and Corinth, up to Thessaly, across to Asia Minor, at Ipsus in Phrygia in the disastrous battle of 301, back to Greece, across to Asia Minor, back to Athens, down to the Peloponnese, up to Thessaly, into Macedon, where he secured power, back to central Greece, across (despite rebuffs) to Miletus, Sardis and Cilicia till his final surrender and death from debauchery. And this is a very summary account of his movements. Or, more peaceably, think of Theocritus. Born and bred in Sicily, he moved to Cos, where he may have studied medicine, then to Alexandria; poems of his maturity seem associated with Sicily, Egypt, Cos, Rhodes, Miletus and perhaps Lesbos, and we must assume considerable mobility.

Or again we have already noted Pytheas leaving Cadiz, sailing up the coast of Portugal, across the Bay of Biscay to Brittany, over to Cornwall, up the Irish Sea to Cape Wrath and down the east side of Britain to Kent, then off again to Heligoland, Jutland, the Skagerrak and Norway. Euthydemus of Marseilles and Eudoxus of Cyzicus explored down the west coast of Africa; Hippalus sailed out from the Red Sea and across to Malabar and the Indies.

The same restlessness is found in art; sculptors were experimenting with complex compositions. Lysippus had produced a seminal statue in *The Athlete Scraping Himself*. This is a single figure standing with one arm stretched out and the other pulled across the body. The result is a transferred cinematic effect: the spectator has to move round the statue because no single viewpoint is satisfactory. One of his pupils, Eutychides, carried the device further in his familiar representation of the *Fortune of Antioch*. The goddess sits upon a rock that represents the local mountain, and this has enabled the artist to give her an interesting posture with right knee slightly raised and taking the weight of the right elbow as she holds up the palm leaves of victory, while the left hand rests lightly on the rock, pulling the upper part of her dress with it and allowing its voluminous drapery to fall in varied and interesting folds. She wears on her head the turreted crown which shows her as protector of the city, and her gaze is fixed upon the distant future. The lines of the figure keep our eyes moving as we watch – vertically, horizontally, diagonally, along the lines of the folds. At her feet swims the young river-god of the Orontes, gazing up in admiration at his glorious queen: we must remember that the great Mother-goddess of western Asia was swift to identify herself with Fortune, and that she was used to the homage of a young consort. Essentially, however, this is a single figure, formally constructed out of a pattern of triangles, but so subtly that again we feel we have not seen it until we have shifted our viewpoint two or three times.

One of the most complex groups, which again displays the search for the improbable subject, shows Zethus and Amphion rescuing their mother Antiope and fastening her torturer Dirce to the wild bull in her place. The original work was by Apollonius and Tauriscus of Tralles, and stood in Rhodes. We possess a late Roman copy which has been adapted to the taste of the times, but the skilful composition must be essentially that of the original. It is brilliant, for it takes the form of a monumental pyramid; yet it is at the same time dynamic with the plunging bull, the tensed confidence of the young men, the fruitless struggles of their victim. Here again the artist has been at pains to insist on a variety of viewpoint; no single view does justice to the whole work. This is a brutal work. Its brilliance is overdone; but it is brilliant nevertheless, and typical of the age. Another brutal work depicts the flaying of Marsyas, who had rashly challenged Apollo. Here we are aware of the individual figures; we do not know about the grouping. Yet the fact that each individual figure merits attention immediately suggests fluid composition – Marsyas, helpless, apprehensive; Apollo, suave, indifferent; the Scythian slave, whetting his knife.

In *Laocoön* we see complex composition applied to anguish. Pliny called this 'a work to be preferred to all that the arts of painting and sculpture have produced'. Michelangelo was present when the

45 Copy of Eutychides'
Fortune of Antioch

46 Dynamic complexity:
The Punishment of Dirce

statue was rediscovered: Lessing took it as the starting point for a discussion of artistic theory. The statue shows Laocoön and his two sons in the grip of the snakes. The composition suggests a Greek temple, vertical, with a triangular pediment, though the triangle is irregular. But there are strong cross-rhythms, created particularly by the monstrously curving snakes, so tautly intertwined that it seems impossible to disentangle them. There is a movement of two of the figures up and to the left, and of the third out to the right, but the arching bodies of the snakes hold the whole in momentary equilibrium. No static stone gives a finer impression of dynamic tension and energy.

The most magnificent example of complex structure allied to dynamic design and exotic subject-matter is the altar of Zeus at Pergamum. This stood 800 feet up on a ledge of the hill, a colossal structure 90 feet square and 20 feet high, approached by a grand staircase 66 feet broad. Surrounding it was the great frieze representing the battle of gods and giants, over 370 feet of superhuman figures engaged in whirling, muscular, contorted, agonizing battle. The scene represents the very thing for which Pergamum stood, the triumph of civilization over barbarism, but where the Gallic monument mentioned later in this chapter shows a sympathetic awareness of the actual people, the altar symbolizes the conflict in clear-cut terms, and the monstrosity of the giants is brought out by their swirling, snaky tails, which offer the artist fresh triumphs of design. There is another aspect of this colossal frieze. In Aeschylus and Herodotus the victory of the Greeks over the Persians is attributed to the jealousy of the gods against the hubristic insolence of Xerxes. Compare Shakespeare's Henry V:

> O God, thy arm was here,
> And not to us, but to thy arm alone,
> Ascribe we all!

So at Pergamum the triumph of the Greeks is seen as a divine triumph. In addition the inner courtyard contained a smaller frieze telling the story of Telephus; the figure of Heracles, Telephus' father, linked the two myths together, and both with the ruling house of Pergamum which claimed him as an ancestor. Ampelius accounted the whole altar one of the wonders of the world; to the author of Revelation it was Satan's throne.

Somewhat different, because a single figure, but dependent upon its setting, was the *Winged Victory* now in the Louvre. The goddess with wings still spread is alighting on a ship's prow; the speed of her movement through the air has caused her robe to cling to leg, knee, thigh and body, and swirl backwards behind her, and the sculptor has caught this magically in stone. In the Louvre the statue is finely placed at the head of a staircase, but the setting does not compare with the original setting in Samothrace. There the *Victory* stood surrounded by water which reflected her. When we recall that the statue was painted – traces of colour remain – the total effect must have been most impressive in the brilliant Aegean sunlight.

Other artists moved in the direction of *genre*. In one of the *Mimes* of Herondas two women are visiting a temple of Asclepius, and admire some of the statues which they see; these include a girl looking yearningly at an apple, and a boy strangling a goose. We have one or two figures of children with animals. Boethus, a Carthaginian sculptor, made one which we know from a Roman copy found in Ephesus, but the child there is a baby and the goose a pet. Another shows a somewhat older boy struggling to take a goose to market. Another boy is the knucklebone player in the Palazzo Colonna. A literary equivalent of these children can be seen in Callimachus' naive girl-goddess in his *Hymn to Artemis*. Sculptors were looking for fresh subjects. One of the most brilliant, known to us from a Roman copy, and reasonably to be traced back to Myron of Pergamum in the second century, shows a drunken old woman; her head is tossed back till the veins stand out on her scraggy neck, and her lips curl in a leer as she hugs the substantial flask to her, oblivious of the fact that her dress is slipping from her shoulder. Or we may think of Pan pulling a thorn from a satyr's foot (in Ostia), or the famous *Spinario* himself. Similar figures are found in the terracottas. One of the finest is in the British Museum; it comes from Tanagra, and represents a nurse with a baby in her lap. The figure is grotesque but human; there is no comic mask. She is fat, podgy almost to the point of grossness, with bulbous nose, large mouth, and chin that wrinkles into folds, a Dickensian character. Terracotta figurines offer a cross-section of ordinary people: a baby asleep in a cradle, another being suckled, a child riding pickaback, a boy wearing a dunce's cap, a fat old man holding a goose, bald heads, crooked noses, snub noses, Negroes, invalids, acrobats, actors, procurers, slaves. Negroes were popular subjects for rhytons and statues as well: we see them making love or music, running or sleeping. Here the combination of *genre* – the familiar – with the exotic and less familiar has a peculiar appeal.

Herondas offers the literary equivalent of these figures and figurines. The sketches are slices of life; the pleasure in them is pleasure in recognizing scenes of the homely and everyday. An older woman pleads the case of a sports star to a younger, without success. A pimp, too smooth to be true, defends himself in a court of law on a charge of abduction. A mother takes her naughty son to the schoolmaster for a whacking. A woman goes to the temple of Asclepius with her maid, who is open-mouthed at all the works of art. A woman is having a love-affair with a slave: he is unfaithful, and she punishes him. Two women gossip together. A wealthy woman introduces some new customers to her shoemaker. A farmer recounts a symbolic dream. It is all as trivial, and as fascinating, as life, and the characters are unidealized, earthy and very, very human.

DIVERSITY AND REALISM

47 Roman copy of an original second-century sculpture (probably by Myron of Pergamum) of a drunken old woman

48 Detail of the central figure from the monument set up by Attalus I of Pergamum to commemorate his victory over the Gauls

49 Bronze statuette of a hunchback, second century B C

50 Terracotta figure of a nurse with a baby, from Tanagra

Naturally during the search for variety some artists found the new in the old, and we can trace a movement properly to be called Neo-Classical in sculptural works like *Zeus* from Aegeira or *Poseidon* from Melos. The most famous Neo-Classical work also came from Melos; it is the study of Aphrodite, now popularly known as *Venus de Milo*. It is fashionable to denigrate it; the late twentieth century has harsher tastes. But it remains a work of compelling beauty, and it is possible to love Cycladic idols and *Venus de Milo* as well. The face is tranquil, Praxitelean in derivation, but with more individual character than Praxiteles gave his goddesses. The genius of the work lies in the contrast between the smooth perfection of the upper part of the body, which is nude, and the folds of the drapery which lies about her lower limbs and which is recorded with unobtrusive and harmonious accuracy. The arms are, of course, missing; one curious feature of the statue is that we cannot reconstruct them with certainty, though the left arm must have been raised, and the right must have been bent across the body. This work belongs to the second century B C. The later Hellenistic age saw such classicizing on the increase. The Roman demand for copies of Classical works helped to foster the mood, but there were adaptations as well, such as the curious representation, found at Delos, of an unknown Roman with bald head, curling lip, and prominent ears, with the body of a Classical Hermes. Less grotesque is the *Idolino* from Florence, one of a group of bronzes designed to hold lamps, and wholly Classical in mood. Another interesting work is Apollonius' *Belvedere Torso*, modelled on a fourth-century original, but with a muscular twist which marks it as Hellenistic. It was rediscovered in the fifteenth century, and inspired a number of figures by Michelangelo, such as Adam in *The Creation of Man* on the Sistine ceiling, and St Bartholomew in *The Last Judgment*. Canova found a type of calm perfection in it, Rodin of restless energy! This periodic return to Classical originals is a curious feature of art history; we meet it in the Renaissance, in Canova and Thorwaldsen, even at times in Picasso.

Another aspect of the age is the interest in foreigners, non-Greeks, *barbaroi*. Classical sculptors by and large ignored them. Typical of the new age is the monument which Attalus I of Pergamum set up in the sanctuary of Athene to commemorate his victory over the Gauls. This is of particular interest, combining as it does an exotic subject with a complex composition. The monument had a round base. In the centre

51 Representation of Dionysus and a satyr in a miniature shrine from Athens, worked in gold and elaborately decorated with jewels. Third century B C

52 Gold ear-ring from Tarentum. Fourth century B C

was a sculpture of subtle rhythm in itself. One Gaul, the only upright figure in the whole complex, has killed his wife and is supporting her limp body with his left hand; he turns his eyes away, and is in the act of plunging the sword into his breast. Around this group four dying figures lay; the most famous is the figure in the Capitoline once called the *Dying Gladiator*, itself even in isolation a masterwork; anyone seeking a comparison of the Hellenistic age with its antecedents could do well to compare this poignant representation of defeat with the impassively powerful fallen soldier from the Aegina pediment. Byron was moved by this work:

> He leans upon his hand; his manly brow
> Consents to death, but conquers agony,
> And his drooped head sinks gradually low:
> And through his side the last drops, ebbing slow
> From the red gash, fall heavy, one by one.

The four figures, on the verge of collapse, faced outwards; they thus isolated the central group, yet at the same time they formed a frame

94

for it, their curving lines leading the eye up to the centre, and then down with the sword. It is a superb design. But admiration for the technical excellence should not blind us to the rich humanity which underlies it. For this is a victory monument; yet it is wholly free from pomp and self-assertion. These Gauls with their long matted hair were to the Greeks 'barbarians'; yet the artist has seen their nobility in defeat. The monument is not, of course, a protest, like Euripides' play *The Women of Troy*. But it displays the same compassion.

A rather different aspect of the search for variety can be seen in the elaboration of the jeweller's art. Here cosmopolis played its part. The spectacle of Achaemenid wealth had come as a revelation; Plutarch tells how Alexander looked on it with the words, 'This, it seems, is what it means to be a king.' The wide outreach of trade and other contacts increased the impact of Scythia and other areas of Europe and Asia. Gold work is more elaborate; filigree is common; precious stones are far more in evidence, and there is a richer sense of colour. We may instance the astonishing miniature shrine showing Dionysus with a satyr, a marvel of gold work set with jewels, or the ear-rings showing Ganymede and the eagle found in a tomb near Salonika.

The search for variety extended to verse forms patterned as pictures. Simias of Rhodes was a specialist in these: we have poems in the shape of an axe, a pair of wings and an egg. Theocritus wrote one in the form of a Pan pipe: the lines diminish in pairs with the

53 Theocritus' Pan pipe idyll, from the 1495 Aldine edition

diminishing length of the reeds, from a complete dactylic hexameter to a foot and a half. Dosiadas contrived the shape of an altar. This last recalls George Herbert, who was also adept at this form of poetry, as also in a later generation was Dylan Thomas.

Another type of variety in verse was found in obscenity. Priapus was originally a fertility god at Lampsacus on the Hellespont. He guarded gardens, blessed the fruits and scared away the birds. In the Hellenistic age he became immensely popular all through the Greek world, and it became the practice to inscribe verses on the statues; these naturally tended to the obscene. A poet who wrote on Priapus and who became known for obscene verse generally was Sotades, a Cretan who lived in the reign of Ptolemy II, and who was executed for directing his talents against Ptolemy's marriage to his sister Arsinoe:

You are pushing the prick into an unholy hole.

We should not forget that the Alexandrian age saw the first of the line of anthologies, literally collections of flowers, begun by Meleager of Gadara, no mean poet himself, who called it *The Garland*, and characterized the poets by flowers:

Dear Muse, for whom do you garner this fruitful song?
  Who shaped this garland of poetry?
It was Meleager, and it was far-famed Diocles
  for whom he worked this keepsake.
He wove in Anyte's arums with many a lily
  from Moero, few flowers of Sappho but all roses,
narcissus from Melanippides, swelling with song,
  and a young vine shoot from Simonides,
plaiting in and out the fragrant scented iris
  of Nossis (whose tablets were the gift of Love),
together with marjoram from Rhianus' incensed store,
  virgin-delicate crocus from Erinna,
tinkling bluebells from Alcaeus' store of praise
  and a dark-leaved laurel spray from Samius.

An anthology is almost by definition a cultivation of variety.

If Alexander was the political creator of the Hellenistic age, Aristotle was its intellectual progenitor. The doctor's son from Macedonia had assimilated much of the methodology of Greek medical scholarship and applied it over a wider field. The Greek doctors built up theory on the basis of clinically observed case-histories. Aristotle used observation as the basis of his finest scientific work, which lay in biology. Alexander fostered this work by sending him zoological specimens from the East. Some of his observations were astonishing in their accuracy of detail: of the catfish for example, which were not confirmed till Agassiz, of the placental shark, which had to wait till Johannes Müller for acceptance, of the cephalopods, in which his observations were superior even to those of Cuvier. Darwin once said that Linnaeus and Cuvier had been the gods of his youth, but that they were both schoolboys to old Aristotle.

Not merely so. The techniques of medicine and biology were applied to humane studies. The basis for a theory of tragedy lies in the plays themselves, and not the least value of Aristotle's *Poetics* lies in his close attention to plays which have not survived. The basis for a theory of rhetoric lies in speeches, in what orators actually do: first collect; then analyse and classify. The basis for a theory of politics lies in the constitutions of actual states, and Aristotle set his research workers on garnering 157 such, of which *The Constitution of Athens*, which alone survives and only in part at that, may be his own study.

Aristotle hesitated for a long time whether to appoint Theophrastus of Eresus or Eudemus of Rhodes as his successor. He finally plumped for Theophrastus, and no one shall say that he was wrong, for that versatile man, though lacking his master's conspicuous genius, was able during his long tenure of office from 322 to 288 or 287 to consolidate the work Aristotle had begun. He was a voluminous writer who had a flair for classification. 'Since it turns out that knowledge is clearest when it relates to objects divided into species, we ought to establish this division in every possible case and manner.' His most important work lay in his botany. He made a clear distinction between the animal and vegetable kingdoms, which even Aristotle had blurred. He established a classification of plants according to stems and branches. Trees are plants with a single stem and branches at some distance from the ground; shrubs are plants with a single stem and branches close to the ground; under-shrubs are plants with more than one stem; and herbs are plants without a stem, 'coming up from the root with leaves'. The volume of *Botanical Research* is of uneven value, and Theophrastus in his passion to accumulate facts tends to accept folklore on an equal basis with observation. But he is a keen and accurate observer; he is not carried away by theoretical speculation; he is free from the sort of anthropocentric teleology which Socrates expresses in the pages of Xenophon, and asserts, for example, that 'the fleshy part of the apple is not designed to be eaten by man but to protect the fruit'; and his treatment of plant ecology and geographical distribution is original and exciting.

The schools at Athens continued their work, but they were ousted from their position of intellectual pre-eminence by the Museum at Alexandria. Here, too, the shade of Aristotle was at work. Demetrius of Phalerum was a member of Ptolemy's court; it is hard to believe that he did not have something to do with the development of the library and museum.

The library was vast. According to some estimates the number of rolls amounted to 200,000 by the death of Ptolemy I, 700,000 by the Roman period. We cannot know; the number was certainly large.

The word 'museum' has come to denote a collection of lifeless exhibits rather than a gathering of living scholars. It originally denoted a temple or shrine of the Muses, a place of inspiration and creative imagination. Perhaps Alexandria contributed to the change of meaning. For already in the third century the mordant Timon was speaking of the 'hen-coop' of the Muses: the Muses (and the scholars) were cooped up in a battery, and expected to lay eggs.

The process can be seen in Alexandrian scholarship. It starts with Zenodotus of Ephesus, the first librarian, who worked on the text of Homer and other earlier authors, and introduced the first critical symbol, the obelus or dagger, indicating a disputed passage. Its great exemplar was Aristophanes of Byzantium, son of a mercenary soldier. He, too, was a textual critic of considerable acumen. He seems to have invented the accent, which gave written expression to the variation of pitch in Greek speech; he also developed punctuation and extended the use of critical symbols. He tackled the lyric poets – he must surely have had a special interest in music – and wrote a whole book on the meaning of a two-word phrase in Archilochus. In editing plays he prefixed *hypotheses*, brief factual summaries of the plays themselves and the background to them; here the evidence of Aristotelian method seems strong. He compiled dictionaries of names, rare words and rare forms. And much else. His work in turn was carried on by Aristarchus, who followed his great predecessors with work on the text of Homer – he was nicknamed 'Homeric'. His fundamental principle, even if he never said it himself, was that 'Homer is his own best interpreter'. All this scholarship was of course useful in providing more accurate texts and more accurate understanding, but there is a certain dryness, albeit an enthusiastic dryness, about it, which is typical of the age.

A good example of Alexandrian scholarship is a story told by Vitruvius about Aristophanes of Byzantium. Aristophanes was invited to be the seventh in a panel of judges for a poetic competition. His colleagues ranked the competitors according to the applause they received. Aristophanes supported the competitor who had received least applause, justifying his decision on the grounds that this was the only candidate whose work was not plagiarized from earlier writers, and proving his points by quoting chapter and verse till the hapless competitors admitted their guilt.

The main academic rival of Alexandria was not Athens, but Pergamum. Scholarship, as at Alexandria, centred on the library, which was a brainchild of Attalus I (241–197 B C). It stood adjacent to the temple of Athene, who was its presiding deity – a fact emphasized by later monarchs, who commissioned a replica of Pheidias' great statue for the library, and linked library to temple by a portico. It was Attalus' overt aim to turn Pergamum into a second Athens, and he went a long way towards succeeding. The association went back to his predecessor. Eumenes I had shown considerable generosity to Arcesilaus, the head and founder of the Middle Academy at Athens, who was born in Pergamene territory. There was also a close link with the Lyceum. Lyco was honoured by Eumenes, and his former student Lysimachus was tutor to young Attalus, and wrote a number of treatises on education whose loss we cannot seriously deplore. (The hand of Aristotle is here, too.) Eumenes and Arcesilaus died in the same year, but the association with the Academy continued, and a number of its subsequent heads came from Phocaea or Pergamum. Attalus attracted a number of distinguished scholars to his court: Sudines, for example, astronomer and astrologer, and an authority on precious stones; or Biton, who dedicated to Attalus his treatise on the construction of siege-engines, an early example of military impulse to scientific research. We should not forget that Athene was goddess of war as well as of wisdom; her greatest title was Nicophorus, Bearer of Victory. More important still was Apollonius. His main work was done at Alexandria, but he came to Pergamum and dedicated the revised edition of his *Conics* to Attalus.

There was rivalry between Alexandria and Pergamum, and in the reign of Eumenes II (197–159 B C) the Egyptian court cut off supplies of papyrus. The Pergamenes therefore devised for their books a sheep-skin preparation, which they named *pergamene* after their city; the name has become corrupted to 'parchment'. This was a revolution in book production. Parchment is thicker and more durable than papyrus; it can conveniently be inscribed on both sides (a necessary economy as it is appreciably more expensive). So the papyrus roll, consisting of sheets glued together at the margin to form a continuous band of parallel columns, was replaced by a book in roughly modern form. Eumenes' court included Neanthes of Cyzicus, a historian of some merit, voluminous output and controversial views; Antigonus ,of Carystus, who had come as court sculptor in the previous reign, and turned his energies to philosophical biography; and above all the Stoic Crates, perhaps chief librarian, who broke his leg while on an embassy to Rome, like the Man who Came to Dinner, and stayed to create a furore by his lectures on literary criticism.

Already in the fourth century the comic dramatist Alexis was foretelling the glories of science:

> Research and you shall find –
> if you keep going, if you're not afraid of work.
> There are humans who have moved apart
> enough to discover aspects of the heavens,
> how the stars rise and set and move,
> the sun's eclipsed. Then of our familiar
> life on earth what might a man not find?

It will be convenient to single out three areas of research and glance quickly at developments in each.

First, medicine. Alexandria attracted doctors, partly because of the liberal patronage given to science generally, and partly because of the unequalled opportunities for dissection in a country where dead bodies were preserved and not treated with disgust. Two of these immigrants attained lasting reputations. The elder, Herophilus, came from Chalcedon, and had studied under Praxagoras. He was notable for his refusal to accept dogma as authority. Experience was to him more important than theory, and he is the ancestor of the Empirical school. His great work lay in systematic anatomy – Fallopius in the fifteenth century said that to contradict Herophilus on matters of anatomy was to contradict the gospel. He identified the brain as the centre of the nervous system, and reasserted (against Aristotle) that it was the seat of the intelligence; he identified the sensory nerves and showed their links with the spinal column and the brain; he gave a careful description of the meninges. He also discovered the rhythm of the pulse, and propounded a mathematical law for the pulmonary systole and diastole. He was interested in the aetiology of disease, which he explained in terms of humours. He was, beyond all this, a wise and witty man with a gift for epigram. Witness such sayings as 'The most perfect physician is the man who distinguishes between the possible and the impossible' and 'Without health, no achievements can be made in any realm of science'. His systematic scholarship marks him an Alexandrian, but his pithy wisdom harks back to an earlier age.

If Herophilus was an anatomist who made contributions to physiology, his younger contemporary, Erasistratus of Ceos, was predominantly a physiologist, who also laid the foundations of comparative anatomy and pathological anatomy. Erasistratus was influenced by Aristotelian scientific theory, Cnidian medicine and Epicurean materialism. He extended Herophilus' studies of the nervous system, isolating the motor nerves, which Herophilus had failed to do. His work on the blood system was very remarkable. It was grounded in error, since he believed that the arteries carried air and that blood was formed in the liver. None the less he realized that the heart is the motor controlling the blood system, and he propounded a theory of the existence of capillaries. *Pneuma*, air or breath, was the basis of his physiology, and he gave a good description of the lungs. He also studied the renewal of the body's tissues through nourishment, on the principle that Nature abhors a vacuum, and gaps must be replaced. He explained disease in terms of *plethora*, a repletion of the body through unabsorbed substances, and prescribed diet, massage, baths and exercise. His scientific bent is nowhere better shown than in his bird experiment. He weighed a bird, locked it in a cage for some days without food, and then weighed it again together with its droppings. From the result he correctly deduced that some of its substance had been volatilized. Unfortunately Erasistratus was also prone to dogmatic theorizing, which limited the value of his work.

It is interesting to note the permeation of medical theory into wider circles in Alexandria. We can see it in the epic of Apollonius of Rhodes. His account of Phineus is a clinical observation:

> He rose from his bed, like a dream with no power to hurt,
> leant on his stick, and moved to the door with withered feet,
> feeling along the walls, and as he passed his joints trembled
> with weakness and age; his flesh was shrivelled and caked
> with dust; only his skin held his bones together.

More notably, in his description of Medea racked by love he says that the pain coursed through her body, about her fine nerves as far as the lowest part of the brain, which shows an assimilation of the work of Herophilus and Erasistratus on the nervous system. In fact Apollonius was a man of wide interests and keen observation. Most interesting from a scientific point of view is his deliberate attempt to study Medea's psychology, carefully based on the observation of the behaviour and even the dreams of young girls in love. Apollonius'

54 Tombstone of Jason, an Athenian physician, showing him examining a young patient apparently suffering from a wasting disease

rival Callimachus seems less thorough in his assimilation of learning, but he too is aware of medical discoveries. In the *Hymn to Artemis* the eye of a Cyclops is compared to a shield with four layers of hide. In the Homeric image the shield had seven layers, but Herophilus had recently discovered the four skins of the eye.

The new centres did not wholly oust older traditions. The leading medical theorist of the latter part of the third century came to Alexandria from Cos in order to study under Herophilus. His name was Philinus, and he founded the Empirical school of medicine. Of the man himself we know little or nothing, but we may judge his practice from the views of the school which he founded. He was profoundly contemptuous of abstract learning and generalized theories; still more of mystical explanations. He directed attention instead to clinical observation and proved remedies. In other words he recalled medical science from speculation to therapeutics. His associate and younger contemporary Serapion, an Alexandrian through and through as his name suggests, held the same views even more aggressively, attacking his predecessors from Hippocrates on for abstract speculation, and claiming, 'It is not the cause but the cure of sickness which concerns the physician, not how we digest but what is digestible.' Maybe, but medical science has proved more effective when it assails the cause rather than the symptoms, and the most abstract speculations have sometimes led to the most surprisingly practical results. Serapion stressed what he called 'autopsy', by which he meant personal experience whether deliberate or accidental, 'history', by which he meant tradition and the experience of others, and 'analogy', by which he meant deductions from parallel cases.

The emergence of the Empirical school at this stage of history is of some interest. Its association with Alexandria links it with the new move to the accumulation of factual knowledge in the Museum and elsewhere; the impatience with abstract speculation links it with the more personalist outlook of moral philosophy. What the Empirical school stood for is summarized in a passage by the later medical encyclopaedist Celsus, in a passage so excellent that it merits full citation. 'They admit the study of causes as necessary when they are obvious, but maintain that investigation into natural actions and causes, when these are obscure, is superfluous, on the grounds that Nature is incomprehensible. The incomprehensibility of Nature is clear from the disagreement of scholars in that field; there is no unanimity among professors of philosophy or even medical practitioners. What grounds are there for accepting Hippocrates rather than Herophilus, or Herophilus rather than Asclepiades? If a man wants to be guided by reason, they go on, they all reason plausibly; if by method of treatment, they all have cured patients. So we ought not to undermine confidence in the authority or arguments of any of them. Furthermore, if theory produced doctors, then philosophers ought to be the best doctors; as it is they have words and to spare, but no knowledge of healing. They add that medical practice varies with geographical environment, and is different in Rome or Egypt or Gaul. If the causes which produce diseases were the same everywhere, the treatment should be the same everywhere. Again it often happens that the causes are obvious, as with ophthalmia, or with a wound, but it does not follow that the treatment is obvious. But if an obvious cause does not supply this knowledge, far less can a cause which is in doubt do so. Causation is uncertain and incomprehensible, and we must look for help to what we know by investigation, namely what we have learned from experience in the actual course of treatment, as in all the other skilled professions. You do not produce even a farmer or pilot by lecturing but by practice. Medical practice, they go on to say, was not a discovery following upon reasoning, but after the discovery of medical practice men raised questions about the reasoning behind it. Does reasoning teach the same as experience? If so, it is unnecessary; if not, it is pernicious.' On the whole this healthy pragmatism, though overstated, was a necessary corrective to an approach which was inclined to be overweighted on the side of theory.

Work in the second century is of less fundamental importance, but the traditions are continuous. Late first-century medical theory was dominated by Asclepiades, who came from Prusa in Bithynia. His medical theory was Epicurean, and in an age when Epicureanism spread widely through the Roman world, his views did likewise, and he attained a great reputation at Rome. He explained disease in terms of atomic theory. The body in his view was composed of atoms of different shapes, and good health depended on the proper symmetry of the body's atoms. Thus blocked or distended pores might prevent the intake or permit the expulsion of the wrong atoms. Asclepiades' cures contributed more to his popular reputation than his analysis of causes. He thought it the doctor's function 'to re-establish the symmetry of the atoms quickly and pleasantly', and prescribed to this end a regimen of physical exercise, baths and massage which has earned him the title of 'the first of the hygienists'. Apart from being a fashionable physician he made distinguished contributions to medical research, distinguishing pleurisy from pneumonia, and isolating malaria.

Asclepiades was the pre-eminent medical practioner of the age. Among the doctors of the Empirical school Heracleides of Tarentum was outstanding. He was a man of wide medical interests and an independent cast of thought. His best work was in pharmacology and toxicology, where he simplified treatment by recourse to the direct use of simple drugs such as opium and balsam. He wrote on surgery, and appears to have experimented with dissection; other books deal with dietetics, therapeutics and medical history. Some of his most interesting speculations relate to the psychological effects of clinical conditions. In Heracleides the Empirical tradition is modified by the influence of Herophilus, and by his own individual outlook. A more typical representative of the Empirical school was Apollonius of Citium. An accident of history enabled Apollonius to touch the development of medical science more than many abler men. His work on dislocations was incorporated in a Byzantine collection of surgical treatises, attended by some remarkable illustrations, some of which had a long history behind them, though we cannot assert that they were Apollonius' own; this in turn made a great impact on Renaissance medicine.

But this was an age of illustrations. Crateuas was court physician to Mithradates VI (132–63), himself an amateur toxicologist said to have inured himself to poison by experimenting with small doses.

> I tell the tale that I was told –
> Mithridates, he died old.

Crateuas' importance lies in the fact that he was the first botanist to accompany his text with illustrations, and this pictorial matter the basis of the illustrations in later manuscripts of Dioscorides and other botanical authors.

One other medical treatise of this period merits mention. After Caesar's murder, Cleopatra returned to Egypt to find herself confronted with famine. With famine came plague, and the clinical observations of Dioscurides Phacas, who describes the characteristic suppuration of the lymphatic glands and the tell-tale black blotches on

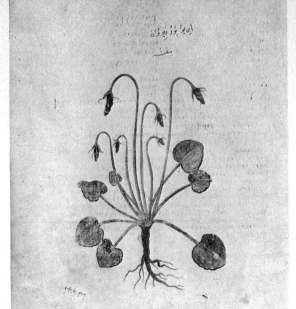

55 Illustration from a Byzantine edition of the *Materia Medica* of Dioscorides, a conscious attempt to impose a system on botany which endured as a standard work in both East and West

the skin, enable us to recognize it as bubonic plague. Dioscurides' work is the first medical treatise on the plague.

The second area of research that claims our attention is astronomy. The first great advances in this field were due to Aristarchus of Samos. We know that he observed the summer solstice in 281 or 280 B C, and his greatest work lay in astronomy, though he was also interested in physics and optics. He was a practical man who invented a new sundial with a hemispherical surface and vertical gnomon. His fame, however, rests on two other achievements. In his youth he wrote a book *On the Sizes and Distance of the Sun and Moon*, in which scientific measurement replaced speculation. He used two different methods. One was to evaluate the triangle EMS (Earth-Moon-Sun) at the half-moon, when the angle EMS is a right angle; the other was based on the apparent diameters of sun and moon and on the shadow-cone during eclipses of the moon. His observational technique, with virtually no instruments to help him, was inadequate for accurate results; but his methods were brilliant. If the diameter of the earth is x units, he found the diameter of the moon to be $0.36x$ (instead of $0.27x$), that of the sun $6.75x$ (instead of $108.9x$), the distance of the moon $9.5x$ (instead of $30.2x$) and that of the sun $180x$ (instead of $11,726x$). The errors were an error of nearly $3°$ in the angle MES, an error of about 20 per cent in measuring the ratio of the diameter of the shadow-cone to that of the moon, and, most seriously, a miscalculation of the apparent angular diameters of the sun and moon to make them 2° instead of $\frac{1}{2}$°. Later in life he achieved an accurate result for this, but strangely did not correct the consequential calculations. In this work he held the geocentric theory. His other great work was to advance the view that the sun is the immobile centre of the universe, and the earth circled round it with a rotation on its own axis which explained the succession of night and day. Perverse modern interpretation has tried to deprive Aristarchus of the credit for originating this Copernican view, but the ancient evidence, which is virtually contemporary, is all but conclusive, and Aristarchus must receive the credit due to a pioneer even though his theory remained a theory, and in the absence of an advanced experimental technique he was unable to convince his contemporaries.

We should here mention Eratosthenes of Cyrene (c. 275–195 BC), in many ways the typical Hellenistic scientist, something of a polymath,

56 Page from an edition of the didactic poem *Ornithiaca* attributed to Dionysius of Philadelphia, another work which attests to the Hellenistic passion for classification and minute observation in science

something of a humanist. He wrote poetry, and was naturally not afraid to show his learning: his poem *Hermes* included an account of the Milky Way and the harmony of the spheres, and suggested what the earth would look like from the sky. Eratosthenes' great achievement was in mathematical geography, in his calculation of the earth's circumference. It was known that on midsummer day the sun at noon shone vertically down a well at Aswan. The distance from Aswan to Alexandria was known as approximately 5,000 stades, or just under 600 miles, and the two were believed to lie on the same meridian. Eratosthenes therefore measured the angle which the shadow of a gnomon at Alexandria made with the vertical at midsummer noon, and found that the meridian zenith distance of the sun at Alexandria was one-fiftieth of the circumference of its course. Therefore the diameter of the earth was a little under 250,000 stades or 30,000 miles. This impressive result was obtained by two miscalculations which cancelled one another out: the two towns are not on the same meridian, and they are more than 5,000 stades apart. It remains a most remarkable scientific achievement.

Hipparchus was born at Nicaea, and worked in Rhodes and Alexandria; his datable observations lie between 161 and 127 B C, one of the most important being a nova, which we know from Chinese records to have appeared in 134 B C. Hipparchus was a strange mixture of the dogmatic metaphysician and the empirical scientist. He believed as fervently as Plato that uniform circular motion was the most perfect, and *must* be the basis of celestial phenomena. But he believed also that the apparent disregard of this principle by the heavenly bodies could only be resolved by meticulous observation. He took two theories of the sun's motion, one based on the epicycle and one on the eccentric, and demonstrated their equivalence. It was more important to Hipparchus that the sun's motion should be circular than that the earth should be central, and by assuming that the earth was off-centre he was able to produce tables showing the daily position of the sun for 600 years. He was less successful with the moon, though his remarkable calculation of the mean synodic month as 29 days, 12 hours, 44 minutes and 2·5 seconds is less than one second out. Over the planets he found his data was insufficient.

Much of Hipparchus' life was spent in securing the necessary data, and he was not afraid to use the observations of others, including the Babylonians, though he was critical of some of the traditional material.

He improved observational technique by practical invention. The finest of the instruments he devised was a diopter consisting of a horizontal support holding a fixed vertical plate with a single hole, and a sliding plate with two holes in vertical alignment. By looking through the hole in the first plate and sliding the second plate so that the line of vision through the two holes focused on the upper and lower edges of the star it was possible to measure the angular diameter. Hipparchus' most lasting work was perhaps his *Star Catalogue*, a careful record of more than eight hundred stars. His most remarkable discovery was the precession of the equinoxes. He observed that one solar year lasts 365 days, 5 hours, 55 minutes and 12 seconds (an error of 6 minutes and 26 seconds in excess) and one sidereal year 365 days, 6 hours and 10 minutes (50 seconds in excess), and correctly explained this as due to a slight annual displacement of the equinoctial points (where the ecliptic and equator intersect), though on the geocentric theory he could not go further. Hipparchus' system was adopted and developed by the great systematizer of the Roman imperial period, Ptolemy, whose work is known best by its Arabic title of *Almagest* (Arabic *al*, 'the', + Greek *megiston*, 'greatest'), and whose exposition of the geocentric view using epicycles to explain planetary movements held the scene till the time of Copernicus.

One other thing must here be mentioned. From a Mediterranean wreck there has been recovered a remarkable precision instrument, equipped with cyclic and epicyclic gearing, and designed to show the changing positions of the heavenly bodies. This discovery has led us to a new respect for Greek mechanical genius. It is some rebuttal of the scepticism shown about Archimedes' inventions, and leads us to wonder whether Plato may not have had an actual working model of the universe before him when he wrote the tenth book of *The Republic*. It remains true that inventive genius was not put to what we consider practical ends.

The third major area of Hellenistic research and discovery is mathematics, in which the key figures are Apollonius and Archimedes. But before them comes Euclid. We know little enough about him as a man. His systematic account of the elements of mathematics lasted as a textbook for more than two thousand years: six books of plane geometry, four of the theory of numbers and three of solid geometry. Euclid was both a systematizer and an original mathematician. His originality is seen in his handling of irrational quantities

in the tenth book. His greatest glory lies in his fifth postulate – Euclid's whole system is founded on a strictly limited choice of axioms (self-evident truths) and postulates. The fifth runs: 'If a straight line falling on two straight lines make the interior angles on the same side less than two right angles, the two straight lines, if produced indefinitely, meet on the side on which are the angles less than the two right angles.' Obvious? Not to the mathematician who desires proof. Provable? Not to a mathematical genius who can discern that it is not. And it was eventually Lobachevski's rejection of the fifth postulate which led to the creation of non-Euclidean geometry.

Archimedes came from Sicily and studied for a time at Alexandria, perhaps with Euclid. But unlike Euclid he concentrated on particular problems rather than on building a system. Plutarch said of his work: 'It is not possible to find in geometry more profound and difficult problems set out in simpler and clearer basic propositions.' The key to all his work is found in *The Method*, a letter to Eratosthenes. Not often do great scientists reveal the inner working of their minds. But Euclid tells us, for example, that he weighed a parabola to get an approximation to the area of a segment; this suggested to him that it might be equal to two-thirds of the area of a circumscribing parallelo-

SCIENCE AND INVENTION

57–60 While not accepting that this was the proper function of his inventive genius, the Hellenistic man of science might occasionally apply his theoretical learning to practical ends. (*Above left*) Hellenistic precision instrument for tracing the movements of the heavenly bodies; it contained at least twenty interlocking gear-wheels. (*Centre*) A slave operating an Archimedean screw-pump. (*Right*) The Tower of the Winds at Athens. Built in the first century B C, the Tower was oriented to the points of the compass; its interior contained an elaborate twenty-four-hour clock and possibly even a planetarium. (*Below right*) Diagrams of a pulley and tackle from an Arabic edition of Hero's *Mechanica*

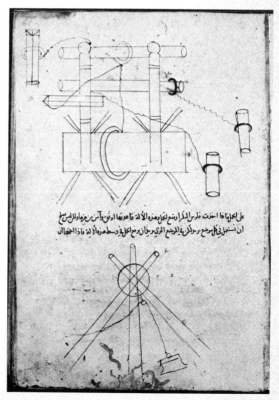

gram, a theory he then set himself to prove. Rather similar is his pragmatic approach to the determination of irrational numbers:

$$\frac{22}{7} > \pi > \frac{223}{71} \quad \text{or} \quad \frac{265}{153} < \sqrt{3} < \frac{1351}{780}.$$

No doubt his greatest work lay in the invention of the integral calculus, which he used to determine and prove the areas and volumes of a wide variety of two-dimensional and three-dimensional forms, including the conic sections. But his genius was wide-ranging. He also created the science of hydrostatics. The famous principle that, if a solid lighter than a fluid be forcibly immersed in it, the solid will be driven upwards by a force equal to the difference between its weight and the weight of the fluid displaced, and that a solid heavier than a fluid, if placed in it, will be found lighter than its true weight by the weight of the fluid displaced, enabled him to solve the question of the adulteration of King Hiero's golden crown by weighing the crown in and out of water and doing the same with equal weights of gold and silver; in the famous story he found the solution while meditating in his bathtub and leapt out naked crying, 'Heureka!' ('I've got it!'). When the Romans besieged Syracuse Archimedes, like later scientists, turned his mathematics to the devising of weapons of war, but he considered this a trivial diversion. The trivial diversion led to his death at the hands of a Roman soldier.

Apollonius came from Perge. His *Conics* influenced the development of mathematics for centuries. He himself summarized the contents: 'Of the eight books, the first contains the methods of producing the three conic sections [*sc.* parabola, ellipse, hyperbola] and their opposites. . . . The second book treats of diameters, axes and asymptotes. . . . The third contains many pretty and curious theorems for the synthesis and determination of solid loci. . . . The fourth book shows in how many points the sections of a cone can coincide with one another or with the circumference of a circle. . . . The last four books are more advanced. One is on maxima and minima; the next about equal and similar conics; the seventh about "determinative" theorems; and the last on some problems so "determined".'

The fifth book of Apollonius' *Conics* is one of the great masterpieces of Greek geometry. His own words show something of the man: 'In this fifth book I have laid down propositions relating to maximum and minimum straight lines. You must be aware that my predecessors and contemporaries have but briefly investigated the shortest lines, and have only proved what straight lines touch the sections, and, conversely, by virtue of what properties they are tangents. For my part, I have proved these properties in the first book (without, however, making any use, in the proofs, of the doctrine of the shortest lines), inasmuch as I wished to connect them closely with that part of the subject in which I treat of the production of the three conic sections, the better to show that in each of the three sections countless properties and necessary results appear, with respect to the original (transverse) character. I have separated the propositions in which I discuss the shortest lines into classes, and I have dealt with each individual case by careful demonstration; I have also related this investigation to the investigation of the maximum lines above mentioned, because I considered that those who pursue this science need these for obtaining an understanding of the analysis and the determination of the limits of possibility of problems, as well as for their synthesis. In addition, the subject is one of those which seem worthy of study for their own sake.'

The very list of Apollonius' lost works shows a great mathematician: *On the Cutting Off of a Ratio*, *On the Cutting Off of an Area*, *On Determinate Sections*, *On Inclinations*, *On Plane Loci*, *On Contacts*, *On the Cochlias* or cylindrical helix, *Ocytocion* (on mathematical notation), *The Universal Treatise* (on the foundations of mathematics).

Conics created the *genre* of exhaustive monographs on a single mathematical topic. It treats its subject comprehensively from first principles, but assumes some mathematical knowledge as a prerequisite in the reader. The first four books deal with more elementary aspects, the last four, of which three have survived only in Arabic translation and one not at all, with more advanced topics. (Kepler knew the contents of book five; yet the Arabic text was not available in Latin till 1661 and the source of his knowledge is a pretty historical problem.)

Apollonius was a great mathematician, yet there is an interesting contrast between him and Christian Huygens. In his *Horologium* Huygens, using Apollonius' own principles and, on the face of it, no others, arrives at the concept of a local curvature for a general convex curve. In the fifth book of *Conics* Apollonius continually comes near to this concept of curvature without reaching it.

Finally we must mention Hero of Alexandria, of uncertain date, a mathematician of remarkable breadth, which he combined with a strong practical bent. He directed courses in arithmetic, geometry and astronomy, and also in carpentry, metalwork and building construction. Among his inventions were an early form of theodolite, the toy known as 'Hero's fountain' (which Rousseau used to collect a few pennies centuries later), and, most astonishing, a simple steam engine.

GIVEN A CAULDRON ON A FIRE
TO MOVE A BALL ATTACHED TO A PIVOT

Let AB be a cauldron containing water, placed over a fire. Let its top be sealed by a lid CD which is pierced by a bent tube EFG, the end of which is filled into a hollow ball HI. Diametrically opposite the end G let the pivot JKL be fixed, resting on the lid CD. Let two small bent tubes be added to the ball, diametrically opposite each other; the bends must be right-angled and the tubes perpendicular to the axis IJ.

When the cauldron is heated, the steam will enter the ball through the tube EFG, and, as it presses out into the open air through the bent tubes, will cause the ball to rotate.

But it remained a toy, and was not put to practical use.

It is interesting speculation why these great mathematicians, who went so far, did not go further. Archimedes was aware of the principle of the moment in his work on levers ('Give me somewhere to stand, and I will move the earth'), but neither he nor his successors for nearly two thousand years succeeded in conceptualizing it, formulating it and using it operationally. To put it differently, if L be the length of an arm of the lever, and P be the size of the weight suspended from it, the moment is the product PL. It was this that Greek mathematics was unable to express, and this particular formula remained un-identified till Newton's *Principia*. In the seventeenth and eighteenth centuries mechanics and mathematics were working in parallel; to the Greek, mathematics was a universal language, detached from practical relativities; this was their strength, but it was also their weakness. They did not think of mathematics as a technique for solving practical problems; they were mathematicians, not theoretical physicists.

Scientific and scholarly studies were subsidized, as athletics had been in an earlier generation. Hopeful historians projected the practice back onto Osiris or Agamemnon. The object of the patronage was glory, since practical objects were limited. Medicine was one area: in Egypt state-supported doctors controlled military hospitals and civic sanitation. There was some support for scientists who would apply their minds to military technology. Archimedes was one, but mostly this was left to specialist military engineers, men like Trypho of Alexandria who, according to Vitruvius, used the vibration of bronze jars to detect sapping. Rhodes, with its rich commercial resources, was particularly strong on the employment of technical experts. The application of practical devices to civil needs was rarer. Archimedes' water-screw offers an example; it was applied to irrigation in Egypt, and used to prevent flooding in the mines of Spain. But Archimedes was unique. The patrons were more interested in spectacular gadgets, clocks, musical boxes, and mechanical dolls, such as Ctesibius supplied to the Ptolemies, than in raising the living standards of the commons.

In general the scholars were supported for reasons of prestige. At Alexandria they received free housing and subsistence, exemption from taxes and protection from outside interference. No wonder that a character in Theocritus calls Ptolemy 'the best employer a free man could possible have'. Ctesibius of Chalcis was asked what philosophy had given him, and replied, 'Free meals'. Already at the beginning of the period Theophrastus claimed that the scholar was unique in being never treated as a foreigner but always welcomed as a citizen.

Learning extended itself to literature, in which the term 'Alexandrianism' has come to mean a combination of polished craft and allusive scholarship. Callimachus was the high priest of this cult. He is at his best in the epigrams, verses of formal polish and controlled simplicity.

> Heraclitus, someone told one of
>   your death and brought me
>   to a tear. I remembered
>   how often we two
> saw the sun down
>   in talk. Somewhere I suppose,
>   friend from Halicarnassus,
>   you are long long long long ago dust.

> But your nightingales
>   live on; on them Death,
>   the burglar who leaves nothing,
>   shall not lay hand.

There is learning in the epigrams. 'Achelous does not recognize the ladles consecrated to Diocles.' Achelous was a river-god; a lover's toast was drunk in neat wine. Or a Homeric reference may be tossed off. There is playing with names, as in the poignant epitaph which may be approximately rendered

> Mr Ryder Senior retired
>   his twelve-year-old son
>   here, the favourite,
>   Victor.

or in the touching words to Saon, Dicon's son, of Acanthus (whose name may be rendered in English as Justus Wright of Thornbury)

> Here Justus Wright
>   of Thornbury in sacred rest
>   sleeps. Death
>   is not for the righteous.

But these effects are seldom obtrusive. Elsewhere Callimachus' Alexandrianism becomes more evident. A scholiast to Plautus tells us that he held the post of librarian at Alexandria; he was not chief librarian, but there is no reason to doubt the tradition. He had an accumulative, encyclopaedic, allusive mind. His works numbered over eight hundred. They show a taste for curious learning: one may instance a series on local nomenclature which included *Local Month-Names*, or another series on the rivers of the world with separate volumes for Europe and Asia; also *Foundations and Name-Changes of Islands and States*, or *Geographical Wonders of the World*. His most famous poetic achievement, *Origins*, is a rare miscellany, and his *Iambics* contain a curious disquisition on the history of the olive tree. The *Hymns* are attractive; the third shows him at his best and worst, for here a really charming vignette of Artemis as a girl-goddess is swamped in a mass of cult titles.

    Callimachus engaged in a battle of the books with his contemporary Apollonius of Rhodes, whose epic on the Argonauts survives. Callimachus' principle, 'Big book big evil', was a judgment of literary criticism and librarianship; to Callimachus the epic poem was a heavy cart lumbering along the main road and the byway of his own concision preferable; better the chirping cicada than the braying ass. To us the two do not seem very far apart. *The Story of the Argonauts* is a series of highly burnished episodes loosely strung together, somewhat like Callimachus' *Origins*, and the parade of useless information is much the same:

> We make for Orchomenus, prophesied as your goal
> by that infallible seer whom you encountered earlier.
> There is yet another journey, indicated by the priest
> born from Tritonian Thebes and serving the immortal gods.
> Not yet did all the stars exist which wheel in the sky;
> not yet was the sacred people of the Danai known to fame,
> though men might ask. Apidanian Arcadians alone exist,
> Arcadians, reputed to have lived even before the moon,
> eating acorns on the mountains. At that time
> the glorious sons of Deucalion did not rule the Pelasgian land,
> when Egypt, mother of men of an older generation,
> was called the Land of Dawn, fertile in crops,
> and the fair-flowing river, by which the whole Land of the
>   Dawn
> was watered, called Triton. The rain from Zeus never
> dews it; crops spring in plenty from floodwaters.

It is tedious stuff; Apollonius feels constrained to allude to all the mythology and all the geography that his reference books can offer. Worse still are the two hundred odd lines cataloguing the heroes at the very outset of the poem; it is astonishing that anyone read further. Fortunately Apollonius has other qualities – and we must recognize in the no doubt select audience for which he and Callimachus alike wrote a fascinated enthusiasm for the new learning which the expansion of horizons and royal patronage had made possible.

Worse still is Lycophron, whose *Alexandra* constitutes an immensely long and tediously enigmatic prophecy about Troy. Nothing, no one is called by its proper name. Heracles is 'the Lion of the three-fold evening', Egypt 'the strand furrowed by the stream of Triton', Helen 'Pleuron's descendant, the madwoman five times married'. Some of the riddles have never been solved: thus we are told that six generations after a tawny reconciler of Europe and Asia, a gallant

61 Mosaic from Hadrian's Villa, based on a painting by Sosus and possibly an interpretation of the Homeric description of Nestor's cup

wrestler would appear, warring by land and sea till peace brought him the first-fruits of spoil and the title 'chief of friends'.

Even the 'novelists' succumbed. Achilles Tatius elaborates on the phoenix or the hippopotamus, Heliodorus on the giraffe. Achilles Tatius on the hippopotamus is not unamusing. The beast is a horse in its belly and feet, but cloven-hoofed, the size of a large ox, with short hairless tail, hairless body, large round head, cheeks like those of a horse, flared nostrils breathing fire and smoke, colossal jaws, gaping mouth, and large crooked teeth. The description of Leviathan in the Book of Job 41 belongs to the same frame of thought.

We sometimes forget that Hellenistic poetry represented for the Romans the contemporary achievement of the Greeks. It is thus not really surprising that Menander was more influential than Aristophanes, or Callimachus than Sappho. It was natural that Catullus should honour formal polish:

> *Zmyrna* by my friend Cinna has waited nine summers
>   and nine winters from conception to birth,
> while Hortensius has published five hundred thousand. . . .

It was also natural that learned allusion became a major feature of Silver Latin poetry. Offer one of the Silver poets a geographical theme, and a full-scale excursus follows: a catalogue of Scythians (Valerius Flaccus), a gazetteer of Sicily (Silius Italicus), or a guide book to Thessaly (Lucan). Natural history is another catalyst. Witness Juvenal on elephants or Lucan on snakes. It is needless to elaborate. Such parades of learning are less frequent today, but learned allusion has not lost its appeal and T. S. Eliot and Ezra Pound offer admirable examples of twentieth-century Alexandrianism.

It was the Greek Parthenius who set the Roman Cornelius Gallus on the path of love elegy. It was natural for Propertius to invoke the shade of Callimachus and sacred rites of Philetas, and pray to enter into their precincts, and Propertius' capacity for mythological allusion stands in direct line of descent from them. Gilbert Highet has told delightfully how, on a bed of sickness, he opened Propertius, and thrilled to its directness.

> Cynthia first enslaved me with her fatal eyes.
> I had been uninfected by desire. . . .

only to be brought up short by

> Milanion, by accepting every trial, Tullus
>   broke the hard will of cruel Iasis:
> for now he wandered mindless in Parthenian caverns
>   and roamed among the shaggy savage beasts,
> and further, wounded by the oak-branch of Hylaeus,
>   he groaned and writhed on the Arcadian rocks.
>   (tr. G. Highet, *Poets in a Landscape*,
>   London and New York, 1957)

This is the impact of Alexandrianism on a mind ready to receive it.

A curious example of enthusiasm for scholarship may be seen in a splendid mosaic from Hadrian's Villa, now in the Capitoline Museum at Rome. It may be taken as certain that the mosaic is copied from an original by Sosus of Pergamum. It shows a golden bowl standing on oddly shaped feet. One handle is visible, and, on the surface of the bowl, the shadowy figure of a man reaching up to it. On the rim of the bowl are perched four doves, one of which reaches down to sip the liquid in the bowl. In the *Iliad* there is a description of Nestor's cup, the exact meaning of which is controversial; and it has been ingeniously and plausibly suggested that Sosus' painting was a whimsical attempt to expound this passage. The 'ears' of Homer's text have become whorled feet; the four feeding doves fashioned of gold have become detached from the cup and have been given life; the double bases, whatever they were, have become figures supporting the handles. But the whole thing fits with the speculative interpretations and scholarly interest in detail shown by the Alexandrian age.   119

VIII HUMANITY

The great catchword of the age was *philanthropia*, love of mankind. It was originally used of the care of the gods for men. It first appears (catastrophically for the hero) in Aeschylus' *Prometheus* where the Titan is twice taunted for the extravagance of his love of mankind. In Zeus' first dominion there was no room for *philanthropia*. Prometheus is a rebel against the old order, a precursor of the new. From this time on the word spreads. In the fourth century it is most commonly applied to the popular, 'human' gods, Prometheus, Heracles, Asclepius or Hermes, to Peace too, divinities who bridge the chasm between Olympus and earth; but Plato astonishingly applies it to the one god of the *Laws*. The Christians later take this up: the *philanthropia* of God appears in the New Testament, and Clement, Origen, Eusebius, Theodoretus and Athanasius (especially in *The Incarnation of the Word*) used the term repeatedly.

The word was already extended in the fourth century by Xenophon and Isocrates to human rulers, and this was applied to the Hellenistic and Roman monarchs. The three qualities they were expected to show were *philanthropia*, love of mankind, *euergesia*, beneficence, and *pronoia*, forethought. All imply that they are seeking the well-being of their subjects. Polybius points the difference between a dictator and a king. A dictator does wrong, tyrannizes over unwilling subjects by fear, hates and is hated. A king does right to all men, is loved for his beneficence and love of mankind, and gives a lead as president to a willing people. The word could be applied to any benefactor: *philanthropia* means benefactions, liturgies, concessions, tax immunities and the like: there are over six hundred examples in inscriptions. Diogenes Laertius attributes to Plato an analysis of *philanthropia* which must belong to the Hellenistic age. There are three kinds of *philanthropia*: affability, beneficence, especially to those in need, and hospitality.

The word tended in this way to retain an aura of condescension. But it could be used more widely. Already in the fourth century Isocrates had laid it down as an ideal for the democracy at Athens. It is used in inscriptions of the relationship of the state of Thespiae with a group of workers, or of interstate relations between Delphi and Sardis. From this comes a regular use in the Hellenistic age to mean an alliance, friendly relations or conditions of peace. Wider still is the Hippocratic principle, 'Where there is *philanthropia* there is *philotechnia*' ('Where there is love of mankind there is love of medical science'). Here we are close to the Latin concept of *humanitas*, central to Cicero, meaning all that makes a man a man; gentleness not ferocity, culture not barbarism, and a fellow-feeling for his fellow-men. The greatest sentence to emerge from the Hellenistic age is found in the Roman dramatist Terence, who derived it from a Greek original, perhaps Menander, and put it in the mouth of a nosy neighbour justifying his nosiness: *Homo sum: humani nil a me alienum puto* – 'I am a human being, and reckon all that affects any man affects me.'

A sign of the new individualism may be seen in the emphasis on portrait sculpture. In the Classical period sculptured figures were for the most part divine. Even when individual humans were portrayed they seemed to have an aura of divinity. There is a well-known bust of Pericles. It tells us little about the man, for it is assimilated to Zeus and reminds us that Pericles was nicknamed 'the Olympian'. In the fourth century portraits begin to appear more frequently: it certainly seems as if one of the types of Socrates goes back to somewhere near his lifetime. Sculptors began to look inside their subjects. Even court portraits by Lysippus reveal something of Alexander. The eyes are the window of the soul, says the aphorism, and sculptors used the eye to express inner tensions – Bryaxis a tender pathos, Scopas passion and ecstasy. Realism was in vogue: the painter Eupompus told Lysippus to follow Nature instead of imitating other artists. But still an air of divinity prevails, and sculptured likenesses were mostly to commemorate the dead.

Heads on coins were reserved for gods. Even Alexander, who commissioned his portrait from Lysippus, hesitated to put his head on to his coins. The prejudice remained strong. Lysimachus did not use his own head on his coins: he used the deified Alexander's. In Pergamum, Macedon and Egypt it was at first rare for the reigning monarch's head to appear. Only the dynasty of Seleucus made a regular practice of it, and he introduced himself initially with the horns of Ammon. The reason was partly political; Hellenistic rulers preferred symbols which made wider claims.

62 A bust of Socrates modelled on the early
stereotype which prevailed before Lysippus

63 Bronze head of Arsinoe II of Egypt

In stone or bronze, portraiture gradually enters. Even here there is
a caveat. The divine types, the bearded Zeus, the beardless Apollo,
remain strong. The sculptors who portrayed Homer neither knew nor
cared what he looked like: they were portraying poetry, inspiration,
wisdom. Philosophers are occasionally marked by strong individuality, but on the whole they tend to merge into a composite portrayal
of wisdom and learning. This is clear when we look at the second type
of portrait of Socrates, which goes back to Lysippus. Individual
characteristics have been smoothed away. Furthermore, abstract
artistic values remain strong: in the Berlin *Alexander* or the Alexandrian *Arsinoe* the individual shines through a strong simplification of
shape and contour; no human face was ever so straightforward and
regular. So, too, as we move through the second century we can trace
an artistic change which Rhys Carpenter has identified as a change
from glyptic to plastic: the forms are shaped and moulded rather than
cut and struck.

Still, with all these reservations, it is portraiture, and very fine
portraiture. The individuals of the Hellenistic age live for us through
their likenesses as the individuals of the Classical do not. We really
do not know at all what Parmenides or Heracleitus looked like; we
have a fair idea of Epicurus or Chrysippus. Or think of Polyeuctus'
portrayal of Demosthenes with hands twisted together in tension,

face drawn and haggard but resolute; Plutarch in describing Demosthenes was describing this statue: 'His face wore an expression of gloomy seriousness; a sense of meditative sorrow was always on his countenance.' Krahmer described the statue as 'centripetal'; the arms are pressed tight to the sides, the clothes almost seem to be weighing him down. This is 'orator' and 'patriot' no doubt, perhaps also 'martyr'; it is hard to believe that it is not recognizably Demosthenes. Think of Antiochus III in the Louvre with the strong intellectual forehead, the imperious brows, and at the same time the almost gentle mouth; this is a character study. Or think of Cleopatra VII, *the* Cleopatra, as she appears on coins. This is no conventional beauty; we might call the features striking, but scarcely beautiful and far from pretty. The nose is too prominent (Pascal's witticism is curiously inappropriate), the eyes too hollow, the cheeks too recessive, the neck

64, 65 Treatment of the full figure played its part in establishing characterization in portrait sculpture. (*Left*) A seated figure of Chrysippus the Stoic and (*right*) a copy of Polyeuctus' statue of the orator Demosthenes

66 Cleopatra VII

too scrawny. Yet this woman knew how to carry herself, every inch a queen. She knew how to make the most of her hair and accoutrements; the famous pageant when she came to meet Antony typifies her dramatic genius. This is a woman of character, of personality.

The advance of portraiture is associated with the new interest in biography fostered by the Lyceum. Dicaearchus wrote lives of Plato and other philosophers, as well as a 'life' of Greece. Aristoxenus, too, wrote lives of the philosophers, which recorded scandalous and polemical material. The Aristotelians were interested in making sense of their subjects, whether philosophers, writers, politicians or men of action: Sotion tried to make sense of the succession of thinkers, Duris moved into the field of psychological interpretation. The Alexandrians took over from them. A life of Euripides, written by Satyrus towards the end of the third century, survives and is of some merit. In general, however, the tendency was for uncritical compilation of all the evidence, anecdotal and apocryphal as well as historical and biographical. The result is the later pastiches which survive as compilations of these compilations, by Plutarch or Diogenes Laertius. Yet they all attest a certain fascination with humanity.

The main interest in psychology is well seen in Apollonius' picture of the girl Medea's first experience of love. What is revolutionary is not the imaginative understanding so much as the analytical observation of the state:

Her heart beat fast within her breast,
like a sunbeam shimmering in a room
as it leaps up from water freshly poured
in pan or pail; from one side to the other
it darts, dancing along the swift swirl.

Like this, the girl's heart shivered in her breast.
A tear flowed for pity from her eyes. Unceasingly within
anguish smouldered through her frame, tore her apart, gripping
her delicate nerves, deep below the nape of the neck
where pain pitiably penetrates, when the Powers of Love
tireless shoot agony into the heart.
At first she said 'I'll give him the magic to entrance
the bulls', then 'No I won't; I'd rather die',
then 'I won't die and I won't give him the magic;
I'll keep quiet just as I am and endure my fate.'

She goes to meet Jason:

Medea's thoughts were single-minded,
for all her singing; no song she sang
gave her long pleasure through and through.
She faltered, uncertain. She could not keep her gaze
unflinchingly on her attendants; turning her face aside
she strained her eyes in the distance towards the path.
Often her heartbeat checked in her breast, when she caught
the passing sound of footfall or of wind.
Not long passed. He appeared to her yearning eyes,
striding up like Sirius rising from Ocean,
rising, beautiful and brilliant
to look on, but bringing bane beyond words to the flocks.
Like this, beautiful to her sight came
Jason, but it brought her anguish to see him.
Her heart fell within her, her eyes
grew misty, a hot flush took possession of her cheeks.
She had no strength to move her legs backwards
or forwards; her feet were frozen beneath her. Meantime
all her attendants withdrew and left them to themselves.
The two of them stood facing one another, soundlessly, word-
    lessly,
like oaks or tall pines
rooted side by side in the hills at peace
when the wind drops; then the wind blows
and they stir and murmur ceaselessly. So the two of them
were on the point of full speech together when the wind of Love
    should blow.   125

Apollonius does not in the end rank among the great poets. But he helped to mould one of the greatest of all. Vergil's Dido is in the direct line of descent from Medea. Servius in his prologue to *Aeneid* 4 says that he transferred her whole, but that is of course an overstatement. Apollonius helped Vergil to enter into a woman's heart and to see love from the woman's side. Euripides had shown this understanding and demonstrated a woman's capacity for tragic heroism. Apollonius entered into the happiness of a woman's love. So did Vergil, but he turned it to tragedy. In exploring Dido's soul he turned some minor points of Apollonius' treatment to major use. Apollonius gave Medea a sister, who furthers the plot; Vergil gave Dido a sister who, as confidante, furthers our knowledge of Dido. Apollonius made the Colchians threaten to burn Jason's ships; Vergil makes this desire the culmination of the hatred which emerges from Dido's love. Apollonius organizes an official marriage between Jason and Medea to satisfy Alcinous in advance, and sets it in 'a sacred cave', with the Nymphs as decorative mythological adjuncts; Vergil takes the cave scene and makes it intense and unofficial with all the powers of Nature participating. Perhaps most telling of all, Apollonius compares Medea's first experience of love with the flickering light reflected from a pan of water; Vergil applies this same simile to Aeneas, sleepless and worrying. This is a marvellous touch; the wheel has come full circle, and our understanding of Dido infects our understanding of Aeneas.

This same psychological interest can be seen in Theocritus' second *Idyll*. Theocritus has been in the eyes of posterity the greatest of the three major Alexandrian poets, though it is fair to say that he tried to do less. He worked on a smaller scale than Apollonius, and was critical of those

> who strive
> to build a house as high as the peak of a mountain's dominion,
> those cocks of poetry who waste their efforts
> crowing against the poet of Chios.

Theocritus quietly built his own world of pastoral artifice. It has little to do with the real life of Sicily, a life of economic hardship, though details are delightfully observed. Suddenly we find we are on a deeper level of understanding, in the agony of a heart:

The instant I sensed him
stepping with light tread through my doorway –
   Lady Moon, recall the origin of my love –
I was frozen through, colder than snow, and on my face
sweat dripped down like drops of rain.
No words came, not even the words which children
mutter to their dear mother as they sleep.
My lovely body stiffened completely, like a doll.
   Lady Moon, recall the origin of my love.
He looked at me without emotion.

There are echoes of Sappho, but Theocritus has examined a real experience, and the ambivalence of the girl's emotions, hating and loving, wanting to see the man in torment and yet yearning for him, is powerfully conveyed.

The sea is silent, the winds are silent,
but the pain within me is never silent.

This was the age when poets explored love. Here is Asclepiades:

A drink of iced water brings delight to the thirsty in summer. The
                                                      west wind
   brings delight to sailors in spring after winter's storm.
The greatest delight is when one blanket covers two lovers,
   and the goddess of Love receives honour from both.

Or again:

The night is long and stormy; it passes before the Pleiads set.
   I pass to and fro, drenched with rain, before her door.
She plays me false, but I'm wounded with longing for her.
                                                      Aphrodite
   shot me, not with love, but a cruel fire-tipped arrow.

Philitas of Cos, whose poems to his mistress Bittis have not survived, was for Propertius three centuries later the very spirit of love poetry. Or we may remember Meleager, compiler of *The Garland*, and his Heliodora:

The garland is fading round Heliodora's head.
   She glows and forms a garland for the garland.

127

Similar in mood is an exquisite fragment of dramatic lyric discovered by Grenfell:

> Our choice was mutual.
> We were bound together. Love's goddess
> guarantees our love. Bitter
> the remembrance
> that as he kissed me he planned
> to leave me,
> bringing confusion
> as he brought me love.
> Love gripped me,
> I admit it.
> Lovely stars, Queen Night, partner of my love,
> deliver me yet to the man to whom Love's goddess
> and mighty overpowering Love
> are leading me, a willing captive. . . .

And here is a love poem from Judaea, which has recently been shown on linguistic grounds to belong to the Hellenistic age:

> I am a rose of Sharon,
>   a lily of the valleys.
> As a lily among brambles,
>   so is my love among maidens.
> As an apple-tree among the trees of the wood,
>   so is my beloved among young men.
> With great delight I sat in his shadow,
>   and his fruit was sweet to my taste.
> He brought me to the banqueting house,
>   and his banner over me was love.
> Sustain me with raisins,
>   refresh me with apples;
>   for I am sick with love.
> O that his left hand were under my head,
>   and that his right hand embraced me.
>   (Song of Songs)

These are human beings, exploring human relationship.

It leads us, interestingly enough, to the novel, the romance, another contribution to the mood of withdrawal which developed in the

67 Terracotta figurine of a stock character, the loud-mouthed soldier
68 A comic mask in a mosaic from the House of Menander at Mytilene
69 A chorusmaster distributing costumes and masks to his actors before a performance

Roman period. Escapist perhaps, but rich in its humanity, and in the tenderness of its understanding of love. A French critic, André Bonnard, rhapsodizes over it: 'Sweet love-story of Daphnis and Chloe, how gracefully modelled on that memory of our first loves that we cherish within us! The girl bathes the boy's brown back and cannot refrain from touching and touching again; the boy's wandering eyes notice for the first time that the girl's hair is golden; kisses are offered in play, sweet kisses with a poisoned sting; love learning to know itself in laughter and tears, vanished sleep and beating heart, a world turned to drabness and the sudden magic of a face; the unimagined freshness of a glance – all the charming, fumbling apprenticeship of pleasure and tenderness. . . .'

Menander's plays finely portray the new humanism. Characters in the Old Comedy are not individuals in this sense: we do not feel at one with them. In New Comedy we are concerned with the characters and their fates. We are after all dealing with real-life situations, with husbands and wives, with love-affairs (Ovid said that Menander is for ever on the subject of love), with rich men whose whole aim is money, with hangers-on who will do anything for a free meal, with grumpy old codgers, with unscrupulous slaves, with open-hearted prostitutes, with much-travelled soldiers given to exaggeration, with cooks of professional vanity, with anxious mothers and gossiping wives. There is here a salutary and humbling truth. New Comedy shows us types, as we know from the representation of masks, which are readily assignable to stock characters, and seldom or never to individuals in individual plays. Yet in those types we recognize ourselves – or our neighbours. The braggart soldier is a case in point. He seems to us a caricature, because the type of the soldier has changed. But what of Adaeus, whose reports were couched in such exaggerated terms that he was nicknamed 'Philip's cockerel'? What of Nicostratus who armed himself, like Heracles, with club and lion's skin? It is part of our humanity that we can be classified. Alciphro in one of his letters speaks of Menander's types, his misers, lovers, the superstitious and the suspicious.

Occasionally, and occasionally only, we meet a character who is not so lightly to be pigeonholed. Demeas in *The Woman from Samos* is one such. Glycera in *The Girl Who Has Her Hair Cut Off* is another, dignified, courageous, independent; her scene with Pataecus is a masterpiece; she has been well compared with Helena in *All's Well that Ends Well.* Charisius in *The Arbitrants* is yet another. He has cast off his wife for having an illegitimate child, overhears her refusing to cast him off, and realizes that he is condemning her for the sort of affair he has had himself. Not merely so: he turns out to be the very father of the child conceived in the dark four months before marriage. But before this is revealed, his flash of insight and understanding and rejection of the twofold standard of morality, by which a man sows his wild oats and a woman becomes culpably damaged goods, is one of the great moments of the theatre. These characters are rare. In real life, too, distinctive individualism is depressingly rare: there *is* a tendency to conform – even in rebellion against conformity. 'Menander! Life! I wonder which of you has copied which.'

The same sort of realism is to be seen in Theophrastus' *Characters*, a by-product of the Aristotelian passion for collecting and classifying observations. The observations are shrewd and entertaining. We do not readily forget the Stupid Man, who can't remember his own door and gets bitten by his neighbour's dog; the Tactless Man who invites you for a walk when you've just arrived from a long journey, and makes a misogynistic speech at a wedding; the Superstitious Man, who consults a diviner because a mouse has nibbled a hole in a bag, receives the advice to have the bag patched, but is more concerned with apotropaic ritual; or the Coward who hides his sword and has to go back and fetch it. This is, in its own way, a minor masterpiece, and none of its later imitators, Hall or Earle or Law or La Bruyère or Vauvenaigues, quite achieved the mastery of the originator.

70 The temple of Apollo at Didyma, begun in the third century B C

The Olympian religion faded. Apollo's temple at Didyma stood un-finished four centuries after it was begun. Zeus held his own, and took over from the sun-gods and mountain-gods of Syria. Dionysus, too, held his own, partly through people's desire for the more personal experience of the Mysteries (which were the subject of a scandal at Rome in the second century B C), partly through the popularity of the theatre and the prevalence of guilds of actors dedicated to him. The great shrines remained great. Apollo retained his hold on Delphi, Apollo and Artemis on Delos, Demeter and Korē on Eleusis, Aphro-dite on Paphos, Artemis on Ephesus (but she was the great Mother-goddess of Asia Minor with a Greek name attached). What happened was that religious belief became diffused with the retreat of the horizons. This can be seen in Queen Stratonice, who was a benefactress of Apollo at Delos and a member of a society at Smyrna dedicated to the Egyptian jackal-god Anubis, and who rebuilt the temple of the goddess Atargatis at Hierapolis in Syria. Or take the dedications of Antiochus I of Commagene. He himself bears the titles, 'God Righteous Manifest Philoroman Philhellene'. His dedications are to Zeus Oromasdes, Apollo Mithras Helios Hermes and Artagnes Heracles Ares, as well as to his own country and his ancestors. Identi-fications and assimilations were the order of the day. Hermes, for example, became one with the Egyptian Thoth and the centre of a new mystery cult.

Somewhere about the year 100 B C there seems to have been some-thing of a religious revival. Athens had begun to send elaborate pro-cessions to fetch the sacred fire from Delphi in 138–137 and 128–127; the latter was the occasion of one of the famous hymns recorded at Delphi. These processions were renewed in 106–105 and again in 97–96. At about the same time they revived the great festival at Delos. Boeotia revived old festivals and established new. All through the second century throughout the Greek world religious festivals sprang up in honour of Rome. In 99 B C Lindos on Rhodes organized and published its religious records. At about the same date Corope in Thessaly restored its oracle of Apollo. In 92 Andania in the Peloponnese published a long decree about the shrine of the mysteries of Demeter and Korē: it covers decorous behaviour, the work and duties of the priests, the organization of the procession, sacred drama and sacred meal, the right of asylum for slaves, the bank and shops, the water-supply, and much else both religious and practical.

The new age needed a new religion. Characteristic was the emergence of Sarapis. He had, seemingly, existed before, though the matter is controversial. His name was a fusion of Osiris, the great fertility god of Egypt, and Apis, the sacred bull. His cult statue was said to have been brought to Alexandria from Sinope on the Euxine; this looks like an attempt to universalize him, like the story spread by the Egyptian authorities that he was found in Babylon. The fact is that Ptolemy needed a new universal god for his cosmopolitan authority. To all intents and purposes he invented Sarapis. He failed in his immediate purpose; the Egyptians stuck to the gods they knew. In other ways he succeeded beyond his dreams. Sarapis caught on in the Graeco-Roman world. His cult statue with its gleaming eyes and golden head was one of the wonders of Alexandria. He took Isis as his consort, and she, too, made the universal claims we find in Apuleius or in the Isis aretalogy; she is the single true form of all the multifarious gods and goddesses. Sarapis took to himself the majesty of Zeus and the kindly healing presence of Asclepius. And thus his worship spread, even to a Roman Mithraeum in remote Britain. He met the needs of the age.

The monarch himself might form the basis of a cult appropriate to the new age. Yet it is extraordinarily difficult to feel exactly what the ordinary citizen understood by the divinization of a ruler. There were three major precedents. One was the 'Oriental' divine monarch, inescapable in Egypt, in Persia offered honours (such as obeisance) which implied divinity to the alien Greeks, but not to the Persians. A second was the Greek concept of 'heroic' honours, paid among others to the founders of cities; Alexander and his successors certainly qualified under this last head. A third was the original concept of the hero as the son of a god, who himself achieves divinity as a reward for his services to mankind – Heracles or Asclepius. Once the principle of divine ancestry was accepted this led obviously to divinization after death though not in life: the principle was clear in the Roman empire where

71 Gold medallion from Egypt
showing Alexander wearing the horns
of Zeus Ammon

there was an analogy in adscription to the senate, and it led naturally to the concept of the divine house, *divina domus*. This third view was supported in the Greek world by the close approximation between the terms 'god' (*theos*) and 'immortal' (*athanatos*). When the Christian writer says that the Divine Word became Man that we might become God, it is doubtful whether he means more than 'became mortal that we might become immortal'. The present ruler was subject to mortality; after death he might put on divinity. But a divine aura might presently attach to him: Octavian's title of Augustus was a brilliant stroke of propaganda.

Alexander brought together all these strands. It was in Egypt that he first began to think in new terms, and his experiences in the East strengthened a decision to be a divine king. As founder of Alexandria he received heroic honours, and four and a half centuries after his death was remembered there as a god and as 'founder of the city and of its youth organizations'. Further, by proclaiming himself son of Zeus Ammon and by associating himself with Heracles and Dionysus – his image on coins regularly bears the lionskin of Heracles – he was involved in the concept of the divine child who grew to divinity.

What was in Alexander's mind is hard to disentangle. In Egypt he could not rule without divinity: even the soberest of Roman emperors could not evade that. It is likely that he saw ruler-worship as a political device for unifying the empire: it was a natural extension of the Egyptian monarchy. It was on the face of it a brilliant device, though, as the Romans found, the limitations of those who came after might bring it into disrepute so that they were driven to a new unifying religion, first in sun-worship and then in Christianity. It is hard to see what other device, political or religious, was available to Alexander.

OLYMPIAN SURVIVORS
72 (*Above*) First-century BC head of Zeus
73 (*Above right*) Bronze head of Apollo,
third century BC
74 (*Right*) Marble head of the young Dionysus, late Hellenistic

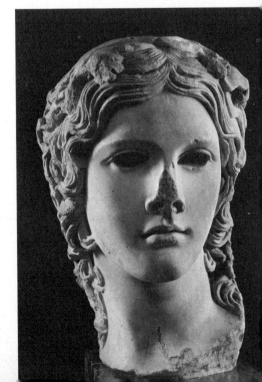

But it would be a mistake to represent the introduction of ruler-worship as rationalistically calculating. We cannot disentangle the political and religious threads, and it is perfectly possible that Alexander's thoughts became exalted by his experiences, and that he became obsessed with a sense of his own divinity.

The Greeks acceded to the demand for worship, but not very seriously. At Athens Diogenes the Dog is apocryphally reported to have grunted, 'Make me Sarapis while you're about it.' At Sparta the decree ran, 'Since Alexander wants to be a god, let it be so.' But the winds of change were whistling through the halls of reason. Fifteen years later, in 307 B C, Demetrius Poliorcetes was received at Athens as a god. They sang him a hymn:

> The greatest, the dearest of the gods
> are here in our city.
> The fullness of time has brought here together
> Demeter and Demetrius.
> She comes to celebrate the sacred
> Mysteries of the Maiden.
> He is here in gladness, handsome, smiling,
> as a god should be.
> He appears as a revelation, his associates all around,
> himself in the centre –
> it is as if his associates were the stars,
> himself the sun.
> Son of Poseidon, mightiest of gods,
> and Aphrodite, welcome.
> Other gods are far away
> or cannot hear,
> or do not exist at all, or care nothing for us.
> You are present; we can see you,
> not carved in wood or stone, but real.
> To you we pray.
> First bring us peace – we love you dearly –
> you have the power. . . .

They actually gave him the Parthenon as his palace.

This was exceptional. On the whole men did not pray to the new rulers. In any event Macedon remained somewhat apart from the other rulers, and only under Philip V do we discern any vestige of the new political religion, and then by assimilation. In Egypt the first Ptolemy moved cautiously, but insisted on his links with Alexander, and in instituting the cult of Alexander he set the wheels moving. He was certainly deified himself when his successor instituted the Ptolemaea in 280–279, though the cult of Ptolemy Soter and Berenice as saviour-gods cannot be traced back beyond the end of the century. The second Ptolemy's wife Arsinoe was deified in her lifetime as the sisterly goddess and the two became the brother-and-sister gods. Their successors in turn were the benefactor-gods: the title, not unique to the Egyptian monarch, is the subject of scornful comment from Jesus of Nazareth. The rulers appeared in Egyptian temples as 'fellow-occupants', distinct from the indigenous gods but with common rights. Athenaeus has preserved for us an extensive, gaspingly admiring account of the riches of a Ptolemaic festival – the pavilion with its 130 couches, its Persian carpets and Phoenician curtains, its bejewelled gold cups; the procession, Dionysiac with dramatic tableaux, satyrs and Sileni (some treading grapes), personifications of the seasons, maenads, wild animals, a silver mixing-bowl holding six thousand gallons in a wagon drawn by six hundred men, ivory and ebony and spices, merging into the imperial cult with statues of Alexander and Ptolemy attended by Virtue and Priapus, and city-goddesses from all over the Greek world, thrones and shrines of the royal divinities with rich gold offerings, all attended by choirs and escorted by the imperial forces. Here we see the Greek blending into the Egyptian.

Much the same was true of the Seleucids and Attalids. The Seleucids did not adduce a connection with Alexander, but traced their lineage back to Apollo. The imperial cult began with the second in line, and the living monarch was not yet fully identified with his divine ancestors. There was no brother–sister marriage as in Egypt, and the queen played a subordinate role, though we do know of a joint cult of Antiochus I and Stratonice. The domains were of course vast, even after withdrawal, and Antioch could not play the part which Alexandria did in Egypt. There was decentralization, and we know from an early period of a priest of Seleucus I at Ilium, though it was not till Antiochus III that a high priest was established in every satrapy; Antiochus II's wife Laodice received a separate, independent priesthood. Priesthoods of this kind did not quite imply that the king was a living god. The rulers at Pergamum had them, but were

75, 76 The cult of Asclepius offered a personal relationship with the divine and evoked passionate devotion. (*Left*) A golden ear dedicated after a cure in the god's temple at Pergamum and (*right*) a medallion of Antoninus Pius showing Asclepius with the sacred snake emerging from the Tiber

received among the gods only after their death, Attalus III was assigned elaborate cult honours, yet still referred to only as 'the King, the divine King's son'. The fact is that the line between heaven and earth was not nicely drawn, and men are not prone to the precise analysis of their religious emotions. We can see the house, the dynasty, as a cradle of individual divinity; we can see also a strong individuality in cult titles which were a warm recognition of the peculiar quality of the particular monarch. We can distinguish between the attitude to the living and the dead, but we should not ignore the religious aura which was attached to both.

It was a paradoxical age. On the one hand there was a tendency towards diffusion, a multiplicity of new cults, a restless searching for one god after another, a strong belief in intermediary powers. This is the age when Heracles and Asclepius, benefactors, near not remote, were exalted; the age when *daemon* ceases to be a synonym of god, and stands for subsidiary spirits; the age when Jewish angelology develops, bridging the gulf between Yahweh and his people, when Wisdom is pictured at the right hand of God. Asclepius surged forward remarkably: witness Epidaurus and Cos and Pergamum. He reached Rome as early as 293 BC, and under the Roman Empire Aelius Aristides shows what deep personal attraction the healing god might command.

This is the age, as we have seen, of *Tyche*, sometimes superstitiously, sometimes as a vital personal force, sometimes identified with the protecting power of the polis. On the other hand there was a tendency towards an actual or effective monotheism. Zeus tended to oust his fellow-Olympians; this can be well seen in the Stoics.

Zeno was born on the island of Cyprus in the year 336 B C: he was thus of Semitic birth, and some have paralleled his high moralism with that of the prophets of Israel, though what we know of the non-Israelite Semites makes this dubious. He reached Athens in 314, for what purpose we do not know, and promptly attached himself to Crates. Some time about the end of the century he began teaching in the Painted Stoa on the north side of the Agora; hence he and his followers were called Stoics. He was a superb teacher, with a powerful presence and a gift for visual illustration. 'Here', he would say, holding out his hand, 'is presentation. Here', flexing the fingers, 'is assent or response. Here', clenching the fist, 'is apprehension. And here', as he struck the clenched first into the palm of the other hand so that the fingers folded around it, 'is knowledge.' Or he would tell the story of the mistress of one of the tyrannicides. She lived a youth of carefree and immoral gaiety. When the assassination took place they called her in for questioning under torture, but she bit her tongue out rather than betray her lover. 'Which', Zeno asked, 'would you rather have? Her years of lightness and love, or her last hours of heroic agony?' With Zeno's eye upon them, men opted for those last hours of heroic agony. His reputation spread to the courts of Macedon and Alexandria, and the Athenians themselves awarded him a golden crown and a state funeral. He died in 264.

Zeno divided philosophy into logic, physics and ethics, as an orchard into fence, tree and fruit. Stoic logic is largely the product of Chrysippus. Similarly, Stoic physics is principally owing to Cleanthes, but Zeno laid the foundations. Nothing immaterial exists, since only body is capable of acting and being acted upon. We may thus see the universe as an active principle, God, identified with the fiery aether and with the principle of reason or Logos or Eternal Law; or we may see it as a passive principle, matter of Nature. As Pope was to put it centuries later:

> All are but parts of one stupendous whole,
> Whose body, Nature is, and God the soul.

The account of God, both in the ultimate principle of fire, and in the doctrine of the Logos, is an 'accommodation' of Heracleitus' thought. The emergence of a world such as ours comes from the interaction of the active and passive principles; out of the aether come the elements of earth, air, fire and water, and a world in which these are commingled. At the periphery of the universe is a belt of aether, housing the divine Beings, sun, moon and stars. The world we know is destructible; yet the universe, being God – Zeno's system is pantheistic – cannot pass away. So Zeno devised a cyclic view of history. At the end of the age the world would be absorbed in the ultimate fire, to begin again exactly as before, with the same joys and the same sorrows, the same successes and the same errors. As everything is corporeal, so is the human soul; it is a 'sentient exhalation'. It is in its essential nature simple, but it has eight faculties. Fundamental is the Ruling Principle, a spark of the divine; in addition there are the five senses and the powers of generation and speech. The soul may survive death briefly, but it will eventually be reabsorbed into its elements.

All the Hellenistic schools put ethics first, and it was in ethics that Zeno was most original. To him virtue was absolute. There is nothing good but virtue and nothing bad but vice; all else is indifferent. But among things indifferent there are some which will be preferred, other things being equal, such as health, and others which will be rejected, other things being equal, such as ill health, and others which are matters of absolute indifference, as whether the hairs on one's head are odd or even in number. Virtue is one and indivisible; it is impossible to possess one virtue without possessing them all; man is either sage or dolt, either saint or sinner; he who offends in one point is guilty of the whole law; if you are not a wise man you are a fool, just as surely as a man is drowned whether he is one inch below the surface or lies full fathom five. Emotions – pleasure, grief, fear and desire – are corrupting, and to be controlled, or rather eliminated. The aim is self-sufficiency, autarky, and anything which stands in the path of this, such as pity, is vicious. Follow Nature, and all will be well.

Zeno owed a considerable debt to Heracleitus, as we have seen, to Socrates and to the Cynics. He appears himself to have possessed a magnetic personality, and high moral principles. Yet Stoicism had one fundamental weakness; its pantheism led to a doctrine of resignation before circumstances. We are the pawns in a divine game of chess; whether we are sacrificed or queened is nothing to us, it is the game which counts. We are actors in the divine drama; whether we are cast as slave or king does not matter, the play's the thing. Zeno's ultimate philosophy is 'Accept'; it could carry men through dangerous and difficult days, but it was powerless to turn the world upside down.

The Stoics swiftly allied themselves with the Establishment. Cleanthes was now head of the school, and accused Aristarchus of blaspheming against the divine perfection of the cosmos. Cleanthes was born in the Troad in 331 BC and lived to be nearly a hundred. He was head of the Stoa from 264 to 232. He was a poor man, who had been a boxer and earned a living by drawing water. Cleanthes made four major advances on Zeno's teaching. First, he essayed a more rigorous analysis of the field of philosophy into six compartments: dialectic, rhetoric, physics, theology, ethics and politics. Second, he developed Stoic physics by his doctrine of tension. Every individual is the product of a proper proportion of the soul's parts, held together by tension. But the individual is a microcosm, a universe in miniature. It follows that the cosmos must be held together and must derive its movement from the tension which permeates the whole, and which is an expression of the divine power. Thirdly, Cleanthes applied this theory of tension to ethics; self-discipline (*encrateia*) is the starting point of virtue, and this itself comes from a suitable tension within the personality. Finally, Cleanthes was something of a religious mystic. He argued to God along five lines: that the ascending series of beings from plants to men requires a best at the top; foreknowledge; Divine Providence; portents; and the regular movement of the heavenly bodies. Cleanthes at times reads very like some Victorian handbook of theology.

Cleanthes' most famous work lies in three fragments of his verse. The first is cited by Clement of Alexandria, and is the least familiar.

You ask me what the good is like? Then listen.
Disciplined, righteous, holy, sacred,
self-controlled, useful, lovely, binding,
ascetic, blunt, for ever beneficent,
unfearing, unaching, progressive, painless,
useful, satisfying, safe and dear,
honourable, . . ., universal,
glorious, without pride, provident, gentle, strong,
longlasting, faultless, abiding eternally.

The second passage has been compared with Cardinal Newman's
Lead, Kindly Light:

Lead me, Zeus – and you too, Destiny –
wherever you decree that I shall go.
Unhesitant, I'll follow; or if I grow
vicious and will not – all the same I'll follow.

Finally there is a longer hymn, full of religious emotionalism:

O God most glorious, called by many a name,
Nature's great King, through endless years the same;
Omnipotence, who by thy just decree
Controllest all, hail, Zeus, for unto thee
Behoves thy creatures in all lands to call.
We are thy children, we alone, of all
On earth's broad ways that wander to and fro,
Bearing thine image wheresoe'er we go.
Wherefore with songs of praise thy power I will forth shew.
Lo! yonder heaven, that round the earth is wheeled,
Follows thy guidance, still to thee doth yield
Glad homage; thine unconquerable hand
Such flaming minister, the levin-brand,
Wieldeth, a sword two-edged, whose deathless might
Pulsates through all that Nature brings to light;
Vehicle of the universal Word, that flows
Through all, and in the light celestial glows
Of stars both great and small. O King of Kings
Through ceaseless ages, God, whose purpose brings
To birth, whate'er on land or in the sea
Is wrought, or in high heaven's immensity;
Save what the sinner works infatuate.
Nay, but thou knowest to make crooked straight:
Chaos to thee is order: in thine eyes
The unloved is lovely, who did'st harmonise
Things evil with things good, that there should be
One Word through all things everlastingly.
One Word – whose voice alas! the wicked spurn;
Insatiate for the good their spirits yearn:
Yet seeing see not, neither hearing hear

God's universal law, which those revere,
By reason guided, happiness who win.
The rest, unreasoning, diverse shapes of sin
Self-prompted follow: for an idle name
Vainly they wrestle in the lists of fame:
Others inordinately Riches woo,
Or dissolute, the joys of flesh pursue.
Now here, now there they wander, fruitless still,
For ever seeking good and finding ill.
Zeus the all-bountiful, whom darkness shrouds,
Whose lightning lightens in the thunder clouds;
Thy children save from error's deadly sway:
Turn thou the darkness from their souls away:
Vouchsafe that unto knowledge they attain;
For thou by knowledge art made strong to reign
O'er all, and all things rulest righteously.
So by thee honoured, we will honour thee,
Praising thy works continually with songs,
As mortals should; nor higher meed belongs
E'en to the gods, than justly to adore
The universal law for evermore.

(tr. James Adam)

How sweet the name of Logos sounds in a believer's ear!

More influential in some ways was the poet Aratus, whose greatest work the *Phaenomena* was commissioned by Antigonus, and probably worked out in Athens. It is a presentation in verse of the astronomical treatises of Eudoxus and Theophrastus, and Antigonus said of it, 'You have made Eudoxus more *eudoxos*', i.e. more renowned. There was widespread interest in the stars. Astrology was waxing, though Aratus was not led down that path. But the stars were important to sailors and farmers, and there had been some awareness of scientific discoveries by Eudoxus not yet available in popular form. Aratus had no original scientific contribution to make. The importance of his work lies in its memorability for people who would not have access to books. Aratus did for his generation what Jeans or Bondi has done in the twentieth century; he communicated scientific discovery to the man in the street. For Aratus is not merely a poet, he is quite a good poet, with command of the literary devices of alliteration and assonance, simile and metaphor, and variety. Beyond this he is a religious poet of the Stoic persuasion, as his famous poem shows:

> Zeus be our starting point; we mortals cannot speak
> without speaking of him. All the streets are full of Zeus,
> the man-packed squares, the sea and its harbours are full
> of Zeus. Everywhere all of us cannot do without Him.
> We too are His family. He's kind to men, shows us
> helpful signs, wakes the people for work, reminding them
> of their daily bread, tells them when the earth is best
> for ox and spade, tells them when the season is ripe
> for trenching trees and sowing seed of all kinds.
> He took it on Himself to fix the signs in the sky,
> putting the stars in their places, arranging the constellations
> for the year, best to show men
> the seasonal operations, for everything to grow unhampered.
> So when men worship He is their Alpha and Omega. . . .
> Father, we call on You, numinous blessing to mortals,
> You and Your angels. Muses of the honeyed voice, all of you,
> We call upon you. My theme is the stars.
> Hear my prayer and keep me from stumbling all through my
>   song.

In other words Aratus takes a teleological view of astronomy. God has put the stars in the sky as signs for Man.

Chrysippus was the third in succession of the great Stoic leaders. It was he who systematized Stoic thought. Hence the later saying: 'If there had been no Chrysippus there would have been no Porch.' Systematic he was. Like Trollope he set himself a daily stint of writing, five hundred lines, and he ended up with over seven hundred monographs. He was proud too: a father consulted him about a teacher for his son, and Chrysippus answered: 'Send him to me. If I thought there were a better teacher, I'd be among his students.' And independent: he did not kowtow to courts.

Chrysippus altered the normal order of study, putting logic first, but ethics before physics. His philosophy is a religious holism: his religious views touch every part of it. Thus one of the Stoic doctrines was that the soul or mind *assents* to a true *presentation*. Chrysippus explains this assent as an endowment of the soul by fate, as natural as it is natural for a cylinder on a slope to roll once it is given a push.   145

So, too, Chrysippus' moral philosophy is based on our *common nature*. 'The law of all things . . . is that which enjoins men, who are by nature city-state animals, to do the things which must be done, and that which proscribes the things which must not be done.' So life in accordance with reason, the moral aim of man, is life in accordance with Nature.

Chrysippus was a determinist. All things are corporeal, though he distinguishes between the active principle of God or Reason and the passive principle of matter. All things are under the control of fate, 'everlasting movement, continuous and ordered', or, more clearly, 'a certain natural order of all things, following closely upon one another and moved in succession from eternity, so that their intertwining with one another is unalterable'.

> If any motion is without a cause, then not every
>   proposition will be either true or false.
> Every proposition is either true or false.
> ∴ no motion is without a cause.

> If no motion is without a cause, all things which
>   happen occur through antecedent causes.
> No motion is without a cause.
> ∴ all things which happen occur through antecedent causes.

> If all things which happen occur through antecedent
>   causes, all things take place through fate.
> All things which happen occur through antecedent causes
> ∴ All things take place through fate.

Such a doctrine seems to do away with free will. If all things are moved by the reason of Zeus, free will is impossible. But Chrysippus does allow some power of withholding or granting assent, though he never really reconciles this with his determinism. He does not doubt that God exists, as the soul (or life) and nature of all ordered existence, much what the new theologians mean by 'the depth of our being', and he does not doubt that all things are in the hands of Providence.

Panaetius was the greatest thinker of the last years of the second century B C. He was born in Rhodes, studied at Pergamum and Athens, and was an honoured member of the Scipionic circle at Rome before returning to Athens as head of the Stoa. His writings are lost but his ethical views are recorded by Cicero. They might be described as Stoicism made palatable to the Romans by a dash of realism. Where

77 Poseidonius of Apamea

the early Stoics had divided man into sage and dolt, king and slave, Panaetius, insisting on the orthodox Stoic doctrine that all men have a spark of the divine wisdom, wrote for the man who was on the way to wisdom. In the old Stoic paradox, if you were not wise you were a fool. If you were outside the theatre when the door shut it did not matter whether you were at the front of the queue or the back. No, said Panaetius, but if you were at the front it was easier to get in for the next performance. To Panaetius the crowning glory among the virtues was justice, not a negative refusal to do wrong, but the positive benefaction of mankind as a whole.

The dominant intellectual figure of the first century B C, and in many ways the characteristic mind of his age, was Poseidonius, who was born in Syria, but performed his lifework on Rhodes. He was a pupil of Panaetius, and shared something of that great man's vision. Cumont summed up his achievement justly and eloquently: 'A native of the very heart of Syria, but naturalized as a Rhodian, Poseidonius represented in all its fulness the alliance of Semitic tradition with Greek thought. He was the great intermediary and mediator not only between Romans and Hellenes, but between East and West. Brought up

147

on Plato and Aristotle, he was equally versed in Asiatic astrology and demonology. If he is Greek in the constructive power of his speculative genius, in the harmonious flow of his copious and highly coloured style, his genius remained Oriental in the singular combination of the most exact science with a fervent mysticism. More of a theologian than a philosopher, in mind more learned than critical, he made all human knowledge conspire to the building up of a great system, the coping of which was enthusiastic adoration of the God who permeates the universal organism. In this vast syncretism all superstitions, popular or sacerdotal, soothsaying, divination, magic, find their place and their justification; but above all it was due to him that astrology entered into a coherent explanation of the world, acceptable to the most enlightened intellects, and that it was solidly based on a general theory of nature, from which it was to remain henceforth inseparable' (*Astrology and Religion*, New York and London, 1912, 47–8). Poseidonius was a traveller; he followed Herodotus' prescription of seeing for oneself. He had been to Rome; he had also been to the fringes of the empire, watched the sun set over the Atlantic, and measured the tides at Cadiz. His descriptions of distant lands were used by Strabo; he himself calculated the circumference of the earth, though less accurately than Eratosthenes, and advanced the understanding of tides. He was a historian, too, and laid down the basis for writing universal history in the unity of mankind. He was an ethnographer, who used the present state of primitive tribes as evidence of the past state of civilized nations.

Poseidonius, as a pupil of Panaetius, stood in the Stoic tradition, and by one stroke changed the attitude of philosophy to the relation of the world to God. The earlier Stoics had held that the world emerges out of modifications of the Divine Substance. In Poseidonius a fiery breath, a vital force, the Ruling Principle, emanates from the sun and returns to it again; there is an undiminished giving of light. In this way Poseidonius prepared the ground for the Neo-Platonists. This doctrine of emanation helps him towards his most distinctive doctrine, the sympathy which under Divine Providence and the absolute sway of Reason permeates the whole cosmos. Yet for all its pervasive unity, the universe is divided: the sublunary world is, as Plato held, perishable, the supralunary world imperishable. Man, corporeally in the former, spiritually in the latter, forms the bond between them. But Man, who is at the top of the corporeal world, is at the bottom of the spiritual, and there is a hierarchy of spiritual powers between him and God. Man being spiritual is immortal, but individual immortality is swallowed up in the general conflagration which is Poseidonius' ultimate expression of the unity of the cosmos. The resultant picture is a blend of Stoicism and Platonism shaped by Poseidonius' restless curiosity and monumental system-building.

In one regard Poseidonius seems very modern. He kept philosophy's feet on the ground. Not merely did he regard philosophy as providing the best discipline for practical government, but he regarded its function as being to provide technological advance. Philosophy for him is equated with applied science, and it is clear that he regarded politics as applied science. One traces the assimilation of Epicurean teaching in Poseidonius' account of human progress through science, but he has made it his own. Man is the tool-maker – tools, houses, the craft of weaving, the science of agriculture, the skill of bakers, the science of navigation from the observation of ships, the potter's wheel, the basic structures of architecture – all these have come from philosophy. Seneca is aristocratically scornful of such banausic views: 'He comes near to telling us that the first shoemaker was a philosopher.' It is interesting to observe how Macaulay, in his praise of his hero Bacon as the founder of modern scientific philosophy, rejects Seneca and applauds Poseidonius. 'It may be worse to be angry than to be wet. But shoes have kept millions from being wet; and we doubt whether Seneca ever kept anyone from being angry.' It is not unjust here to see Poseidonius as the ancestor of the Marxists.

We shall not do wrong if we see the religious culmination of the Hellenistic age in two religions which emerged under the Roman Empire.

One was Christianity. It began as a Jewish sect, but from the first contained the seeds of something wider. Its founder, Jesus of Nazareth, was a Jewish rabbi, but he grew up in 'Galilee of the Gentiles', was interested in the people of the Greek Decapolis, went out of his way to go through Gentile territory between Tyre and Galilee, had among his disciples a Greek-speaking Greek with a Greek name from a Hellenized town, Philip, welcomed some Greeks as the promise of the coming harvest, commended the faith of a Roman soldier, spoke a parable against Jewish exclusiveness. Himself non-violent, he was executed by the Romans under pressure from the Jewish Establishment for political subversiveness. His followers declared that after his execution and burial he still appeared to them and they knew the power of his presence. His vision was followed up by Paul of Tarsus, who took two momentous steps, first in going outside the synagogue to look for converts, and then by crossing into Europe. Paul more than any other ensured that Christianity became a universal religion, the religion of cosmopolis. 'In Christ there is no Jew or Greek, no slave or free, no male or female, for you are all one in Christ Jesus.'

The appeal of Christianity to the Hellenistic world is thus easy to see. It combined monotheism with a mediator. It held to the one God of the Jews, but proclaimed that he was revealed in Jesus; more, Paul, finding an altar inscribed TO THE UNKNOWN GOD (or something similar), was prepared to assert 'I proclaim to you the God whom you are worshipping in ignorance.' It combined the Stoic sense of religious duty with Epicurean compassion, pacifism and friendship. Its ethic, based on love (*agapē*, virtually a new word), meant the constant, patient seeking of the well-being of the other no matter what he might do. This was a universalist ethic, and one of the greatest Christian thinkers, Origen (though not all regarded him as orthodox), looked forward to the day when all, including the devil, might be saved.

The other was Neo-Platonism. It did not emerge fully fledged until the third century A D, though the way was prepared by a revival of Pythagoreanism stretching back to the first century B C. Its great exemplar was Plotinus, who lived from 204 till 270 in the most troubled era of Roman history. Mystic and friend of emperors, lover of children and pastor to his friends, he seems to have been one of those men of antiquity whom one would rejoice to meet. Plotinus was a Platonist who had been through the disquieting strands of the Hellenistic search for quietude, returned to Plato, and sifted from Plato all that referred to eternity, to mould from it a system of his own. His thought centres on the One, the ultimate, It rather than He, beyond personality, beyond existence, the source and ground of all existence. From the One flows a series of emanations – *Nous*, the Divine Intellect, linked to the One in apprehension but not comprehension, thinking itself (like Aristotle's Unmoved Mover), containing the perfect Platonic Forms of all things, classes and individuals; the World-Soul, the link between *Nous* and the world of Nature. So the light streams out from the One, dimming and fading as it passes, and the darkness beyond is matter, the principle of Evil, yet itself negative not positive, the absence of Good. Plotinus in this way can assert that though matter is totally evil, the material world is not, but evil and good are mingled together in it. Individuals count for Plotinus: his addition of the Forms of individuals to Plato's scheme is noteworthy. The highest destiny of the individual is the ascent of the soul, through Eros (Love, Aspiration), to the mystical vision of the One, the flight of the alone to the alone.

Neo-Platonism is in some ways a consummation of, in some ways a reaction against, Hellenistic religious thought. But it was through Neo-Platonism above all that later Greek thought passed on to posterity. First through the Christians at the very end of the Roman Empire, Augustine and Boethius, and that mystical treatise attributed to Dionysius the Areopagite, which gained currency in the church because of its attribution, although it is sheer Neo-Platonism. Then through the Arabs, who picked up a Neo-Platonic treatise passing under the name of *The Theology of Aristotle*, and called upon their creative intellectual genius in the attempt to reconcile this with the genuine works of Aristotle and both with the Qur'an. Finally in the Renaissance through Pico della Mirandola and Marsilio Ficino, in a movement which penetrates thought, education, religion, literature and art. Botticelli and Michelangelo are incomprehensible without Neo-Platonism as the dictionary.

These strands have been interwoven, in and out, ever since. The specifically Christian ethic has been displaced by Stoicism mediated through Cicero. Galsworthy once said that the average Englishman was a Confucian not a Christian. It would be truer to hear the voice Jerome heard: 'You are a Ciceronian' – and ethically that meant Stoic. The Hellenistic age is still with us. We are still seeking for cosmopolis – in thought and life.

X THE HERITAGE OF HELLENISM

Classical Greece gave to the world a view of life which was founded upon the twin pillars of rationalism and beauty. The Greeks asked questions. 'Their methods in science and philosophy might be very faulty, and their conclusions often absurd,' wrote S. H. Butcher, 'but they had that fearlessness of intellect which is the first condition of seeing truly.' Herodotus called his account of the wars between Greeks and Persians and the events which led up to them *historiai*, investigations or questions. The Greek doctors were not content to be told that epilepsy was the Sacred Disease, due to divine visitation; they asked questions about it. The life of Socrates was a continuous process of questioning. 'The Greeks then', said Sir Richard Livingstone in a too romantic book, 'were the first to conceive the idea of civilization and of progress based on human effort and advancing knowledge', and the judgment in itself can stand. The Greeks had that divine unfaith which has also moved mountains.

Alongside rationalism stood the ideal of beauty. In the essay which he contributed to *The Legacy of Greece* Gilbert Murray said pertinently that if you dig about, say, the Roman Wall, you will find objects of interest, but if you dig about any Greek site you will find objects of beauty. And this beauty is not to be dissociated from the rationalism. It is beauty of structure rather than of ornament. In his well-known essay entitled 'The Lamps of Greek Art' in the same collection, Percy Gardner identified as the features of Greek art: Humanism, Simplicity, Balance and Measure, Naturalism, Idealism, Patience, Joy, Fellowship.

This approach is unfashionable today. Modern scholars have said that if we are to understand the Greeks we must see the whole picture, the irrationalism as well as the rationalism, the residual superstition as well as the emergent humanism, the corruption as well as the integrity, the hovels as well as the Acropolis, the slavery as well as the freedom, the interaction of oppressive and liberal forces. This is right. To understand the Greeks we must see them whole and see them honestly. But these are not the things which make them worth studying. Plenty of people have been irrational and superstitious and corrupt. What makes the Greeks worth our time is their intellectual, and their literary and artistic, achievements.

The centre of this achievement was Athens. This city about the size of Leicester or Miami saw between 470 and 350 BC an extraordinary flowering of genius: in tragic drama Aeschylus, Sophocles and Euripides; in comic drama Aristophanes; in history Herodotus (a foreigner) and Thucydides; in political oratory Pericles and Demosthenes; in the development of thought Socrates, Plato and Aristotle (another foreigner); in architecture Ictinus, creator of the Parthenon; in sculpture Pheidias and Praxiteles; as well as outstanding vase-painters, whose names we often do not know.

The achievement, which was not confined to Athens, was linked with the political structure of the polis, the city-state.

The Hellenistic age preserved, diffused and transmitted this achievement. Through diffusion it changed, not essentially, but in emphasis, in balance.

The greatest change was associated with Alexander's flinging back the horizons.

This meant a political change. The city-state was no longer self-sufficient. It had to find its being within a world empire. And it did. The political secret of the Hellenistic age was to retain the values of the city-state within a large dominion, to blend centralization and de-centralization, to combine the positive values of a large political unit with a strong sense of local responsibility.

It meant psychological changes. If the city-state was no longer self-sufficient the individual was thrust back upon himself. The old 'tribal order' had given way to the polis. Now the polis as he knew it had gone. He felt isolated. Hence individualism, and the outbreak of philosophies of non-attachment.

It meant artistic changes. The artist or writer was no longer working within the framework of the city-state. Hence the restless search for variety, for new themes in the homely or the exotic, for the miniature or the monumental, for the exploration of the inner personality.

It meant changes of language, since the old dialects were unsuited to world communication. Hence the *koinē*, less sharp than its predecessors, but of broader use.

It meant changes of religion. The religion of the city-state was not suited to the new world. Hence the political religion of ruler-worship, the invention of Sarapis, the comprehensive claims of Isis, the new monotheism in the name of Zeus, the exaltation of the sun. Hence, too, religions of salvation to meet the new individualism. And Christianity scooping the pool in meeting both needs.

But through all this the contributions of Classical Greece were preserved. Except in science there were fewer individuals of conspicuous genius. But the values were not lost. To transmit is to transmute, to modify, not to abandon. The intellectual curiosity, the exploration of literary and artistic expression remained, to fire fresh scientific and artistic achievements whenever men have renewed their contacts with the Greeks.

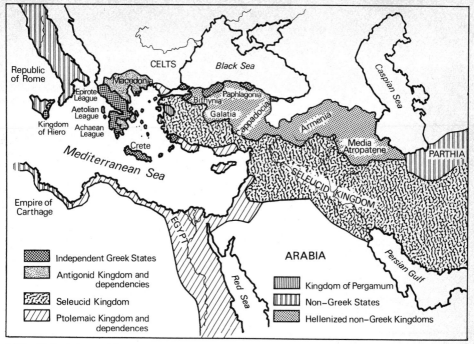

Independent Greek States

Antigonid Kingdom and
dependencies

Seleucid Kingdom

Ptolemaic Kingdom and
dependences

Kingdom of Pergamum

Non-Greek States

Hellenized non-Greek Kingdoms

I The Hellenistic world, 240 BC

II The Hellenistic world, 185 BC

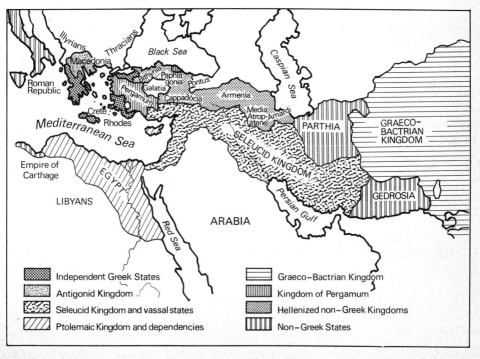

Independent Greek States

Antigonid Kingdom

Seleucid Kingdom and vassal states

Ptolemaic Kingdom and dependencies

Graeco-Bactrian Kingdom

Kingdom of Pergamum

Hellenized non-Greek Kingdoms

Non-Greek States

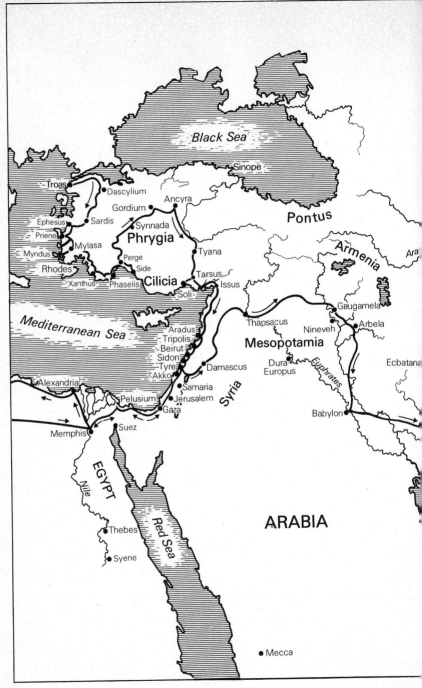

III Alexander's journey

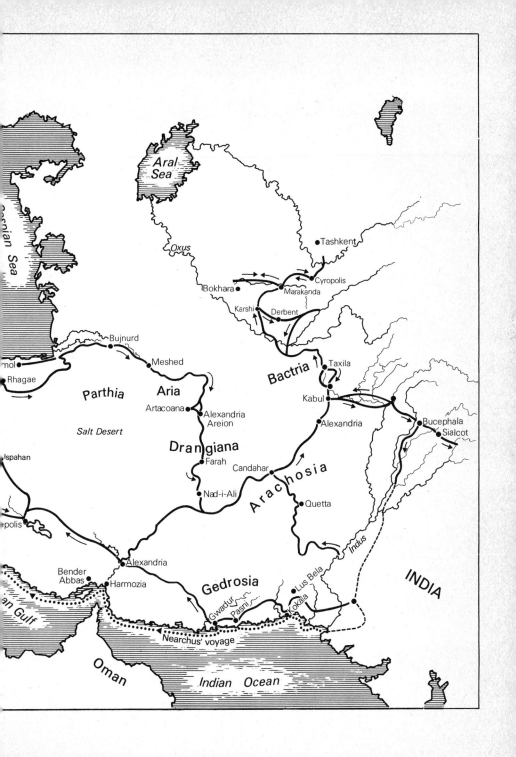

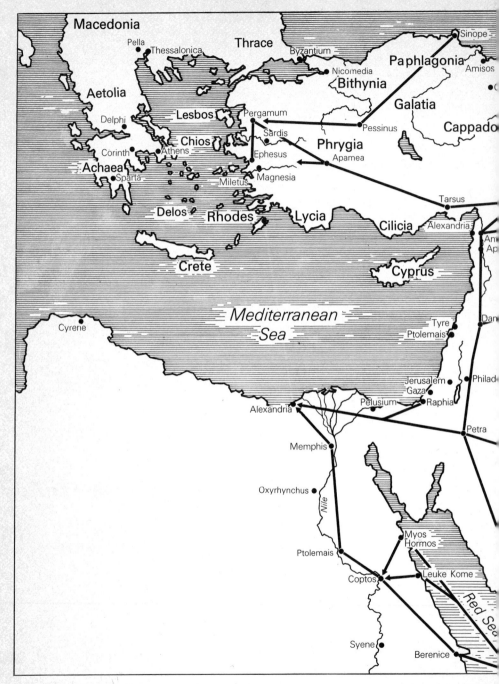

IV Hellenistic trade routes

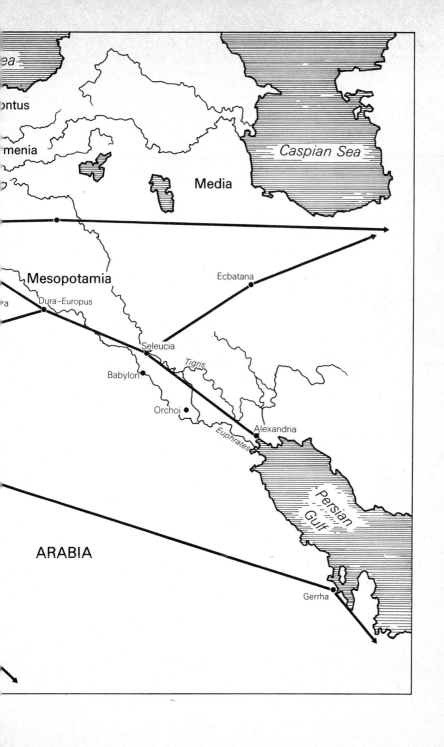

V The Roman world under Augustus

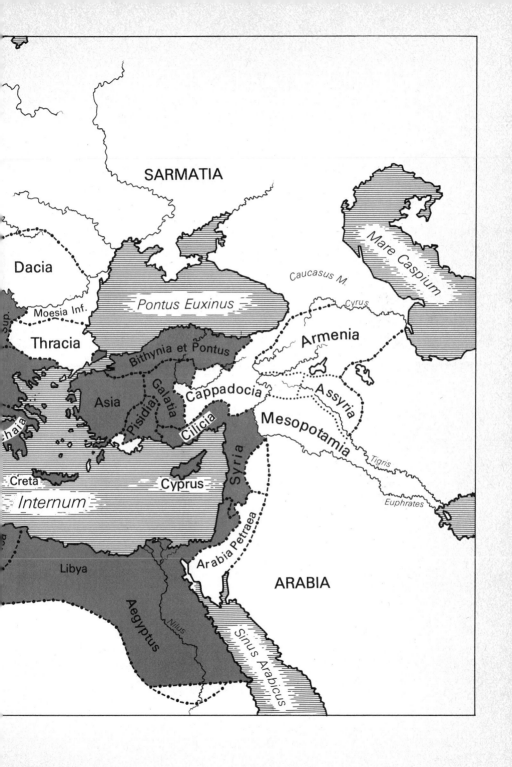

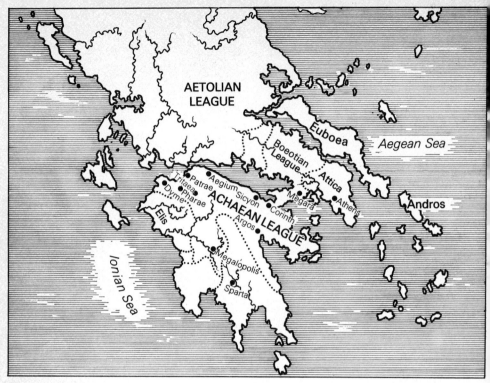

VI The Achaean League

BIBLIOGRAPHY

GENERAL WORKS

M. Bieber, *The Sculpture of the Hellenistic Age* (New York 1955).

J. B. Bury etc., *The Hellenistic Age* (Cambridge 1925).

J. Charbonneaux, R. Martin, F. Villard, *Grèce Hellénistique* (Paris 1970).

W. von Christ, W. Schmidt and O. Stählin, *Geschichte der griechischen Literatur*, Part II (6th ed. Munich 1924).

J. G. Droysen, *Geschichte des Hellenismus* (2nd ed. Gotha 1877).

W. S. Ferguson, *Hellenistic Athens* (London 1911).

T. Fyfe, *Hellenistic Architecture* (Cambridge 1936).

M. Hadas, *Hellenistic Culture* (New York 1959).

P. Jouguet, *L'impérialisme macédoine et l'hellénization de l'Orient* (Paris 1961).

A. Körte, *Die Hellenistische Dichtung* (2nd ed. Stuttgart 1960).

H. I. Marrou, *History of Education in Antiquity* (Eng. transl. 3rd ed. London 1956).

J. U. Powell and E. A. Barber, *New Chapters in the History of Greek Literature* (Oxford 1925).

M. Rostovtzeff, *A Social and Economic History of the Hellenistic World* (3 vols. Oxford 1941).

F. Susemihl, *Geschichte der griechischen Literatur in der Alexandrinezeit* (Leipzig 1891–92).

W. W. Tarn and G. T. Griffith, *Hellenistic Civilization* (3rd ed. London 1952).

C. J. de Vogel, *Greek Philosophy: A Collection of Texts*, vol. III (2nd ed. Leiden 1964).

T. B. L. Webster, *Hellenistic Poetry and Art* (London 1964).

P. Wendland, *Die hellenistisch-römische Kultur* (3rd ed. Tübingen 1912).

U. von Wilamowitz-Moellendorf, *Hellenistische Dichtung in der Zeit von Kallimachos* (2 vols. Berlin 1926).

E. Will, *Histoire Politique du Monde Hellénistique* (2 vols. Nancy 1966–67).

I COSMOPOLIS

FOR THE HISTORY SEE CONVENIENTLY:

Cambridge Ancient History, vol. VII (Cambridge 1928).

M. Cary, *A History of the Greek World 323–146 B.C.* (2nd ed. London 1951).

F. W. Walbank, *A Historical Commentary on Polybius* (3 vols. Oxford 1957–68).

FOR ALEXANDER:

R. Andreotti, 'Die Weltmonarchie Alexanders Grossen in Uberlieferung und geschichtlicher Wirklichkeit', in *Saeculum*, 1957, 120 ff.

E. Badian, 'Alexander the Great and the Unity of Mankind', in *Historia*, 1958, 425 ff.

P. Cloché, *Alexandre le Grand et les essais de fusion entre l'Occident gréco-macédoine et l'Orient* (Neuchâtel *c.* 1954).

G. T. Griffith, *Alexander the Great: The Main Problems* (Cambridge 1966).

W. W. Tarn, *Alexander the Great* (2 vols. Cambridge 1948).

FOR THE SUCCESSORS:

H. I. Bell, *Egypt from Alexander the Great to the Arab conquest* (Oxford 1948).

E. R. Bevan, *The House of Seleucus* (London 1902).

E. Bikerman, *Institutions des Séleucides* (Paris 1938).

A. Bouché-Leclerq, *Histoire des Lagides* (Paris 1903–7).

——, *Histoire des Séleucides* (Paris 1913).

E. V. Hansen, *The Attalids of Pergamum* (New York 1947).

P. Jouguet, *L'Égypte ptolémaique* (Paris 1933).

W. W. Tarn, *Antigonus Gonatas* (Oxford 1913).

F. W. Walbank, *Philip V of Macedon* (Cambridge 1940).

FOR BACTRIA:

A. K. Narain, *The Indo-Greeks* (Oxford 1957).

A. M. Simonetta, 'A New Essay on the Indo-Greeks', in *East and West*, 1958, 154 ff.

W. W. Tarn, *The Greeks in Bactria and India* (2nd ed. Cambridge 1951).

R. E. M. Wheeler, *Flames Over Persepolis* (London 1968).

G. Woodcock, *The Greeks in India* (London 1966).

FOR THE ROMAN SETTLEMENT:

E. Badian, *Foreign Clientelae* (Oxford 1958).

——, *Roman Imperialism in the Late Republic* (2nd ed. Oxford 1968).

G. Cardinali and G. Niccolini, in *Studi Storice per l'antichita classica*, vol. III, 1910.

M. Holleaux, *Rome, la Grèce et les monarchies hellénistiques au troisième siècle avant J.C.* (Paris 1921).

FOR THE JEWS:

S. W. Baron, *A Social and Religious History of the Jews*, vol. I (New York 1952).

E. R. Goodenough, *Jewish Symbols in the Greco-Roman Period* (12 vols. New York 1953–65).

H. M. Kallen, *The Book of Job as a Greek Tragedy* (New York 1918).

164

S. Lieberman, *Greek in Jewish Palestine* (New York 1942).

——, *Hellenism in Jewish Palestine* (New York 1950).

V. Tcherikover, *Hellenistic Civilization and the Jews* (Philadelphia and Jerusalem 1959).

FOR THE MERCENARIES:

G. T. Griffith, *The Mercenaries of the Hellenistic World* (Cambridge 1935).

M. Launey, *Recherches sur les armées Hellénistiques* (Paris 1950).

FOR SCULPTURES:

G. M. A. Richter, *Three Critical Periods of Greek Sculpture* (Oxford 1951).

FOR THE HISTORIANS:

J. Ferguson, 'Ancient Historiography', in *Phrontisterion*, 1966, 1–12.

FOR ALEXANDRIA:

E. Badian, 'Ancient Alexandria', in *Studies in Greek and Roman History* (Oxford 1964).

E. N. Borza, 'Alexander and the Return from Siwa', in *Historia*, 1967, 369.

E. Breccia, *Alexandrea ad Aegyptum* (Bergamo 1922).

E. M. Forster, *Alexandria* (New York 1961).

E. A. Parsons, *The Alexandrian Library* (London 1952).

C. Préaux, 'Alexandria under the Ptolemies', in A. Toynbee, *Cities of Destiny* (London 1967).

A. Rowe, *Discovery of the Famous Temple and Enclosure of Sarapis at Alexandria*, Supplément aux *Annales du Service des Antiquités de l'Egypte*, cahier no. 2 (Cairo 1946).

C. B. Welles, 'The Discovery of Sarapis and the Foundation of Alexandria', in *Historia*, 1962, 271–98.

FOR 'KOINE':

B. F. C. Atkinson, *The Greek Language* (2nd ed. London 1931).

K. Brugmann and E. Schwyzer, *Griechische Grammatik* (Munich 1953).

P. S. Costas, *An Outline of the History of the Greek Language* (Chicago 1936).

A. Deissmann, *Bible Studies* (Eng. transl. 2nd ed. Edinburgh 1903).

J. H. Moulton, *A Grammar of New Testament Greek* (3rd ed. Edinburgh 1967).

L. Radermacher, 'Koine', in *Sitzungsberichte der Akademie der Wissenschaften*, Vienna, 224.

FOR THE UNITY OF MANKIND:

H. C. Baldry, *The Unity of Mankind in Greek Thought* (Cambridge 1965).

FOR THIS VIEW OF CHRISTIANITY:
J. Ferguson, 'Athens and Jerusalem', in *Religious Studies*, 1972, 1–13.

II POLIS

V. H. Ehrenberg, *The Greek State* (2nd ed. London 1969).

E. A. Freeman, *History of Federal Government*, vol. 1 (London 1863).

M. Hammond, *City-State and World-State in Greek and Roman Political Thought until Augustus* (Cambridge, Mass. 1955).

A. H. M. Jones, *The Cities of the Eastern Roman Provinces* (2nd ed. Oxford 1971).

——, *The Greek City from Alexander to Justinian* (Oxford 1940).

J. A. O. Larsen, *Greek Federal States* (Oxford 1968).

——, *Representative Government in Greek and Roman History* (Berkeley and Los Angeles 1955).

F. W. Walbank, *Aratus of Sicyon* (Cambridge 1933).

C. B. Welles, *Royal Correspondence in the Hellenistic Period* (New Haven 1934).

R. E. Wycherley, *How the Greeks Built Cities* (London 1949).

FOR CLEARCHUS:
Comptes-Rendus de l'Académie des Inscriptions et Belles-Lettres, 1967, 281–97, 306–24; 1968, 263–79, 415–58.

III WAYS AND MEANS

Rhys Carpenter, *Beyond the Pillars of Heracles* (New York 1966).

M. Cary and E. H. Warmington, *The Ancient Explorers* (London 1929).

L. Casson, *The Ancient Mariners* (London 1959).

J. Day, *An Economic History of Athens under Roman Domination* (New York 1942).

C. Edgar, *Zenon Papyri in the University of Michigan Collection* (Michigan 1931).

M. I. Finley (ed.), *Slavery in the Ancient World* (Cambridge 1960).

G. Glotz, *Ancient Greece at Work* (Eng. transl. London 1926).

F. M. Heichelheim, *An Ancient Economic History*, vol. III (Leyden 1970).

U. Kahrstedt, *Geschichte des griechisch-römischen Altertums* (Munich 1949).

C. Préaux, *L'économie royale des Lagides* (Brussels 1939).

M. Rostovtzeff, *A Large Estate in Egypt in the Third Century B.C.* (Madison 1922).

——, *The Social and Economic History of the Hellenistic World* (3 vols. Oxford 1941).

J. Toutain, *The Economic Life of the Ancient World* (London 1930).

W. L. Westermann, *Upon Slavery in Ptolemaic Egypt* (New York 1929).

IV UTOPIA

This is a controversial topic which I hope to treat in a full-length book. Recent interpreters tend to be more sceptical about the relation of theory to practice. I was introduced to the subject by M. P. Charlesworth.

IN GENERAL:
W. W. Tarn, *Alexander the Great*, vol. II, appendix 25 (Cambridge 1948).
M. Finley, 'Utopianism Ancient and Modern', in K. H. Wolff and B. Moore Jnr, *The Critical Spirit* (Boston 1967).

FOR ZENO:
H. C. Baldry, 'Zeno's Ideal State', *Journal of Hellenic Studies*, 1959, 3–15.

ON STOIC INFLUENCE:
J. Bidez, 'La Cité du Monde et la Cité du Soleil chez les Stoiciens', in *Bulletin de l'Académie Royale de Belgique* (Lettres), 5th ed., 1932, 244 ff.

FOR CLEOMENES:
T. W. Africa, *Phylarchus and the Spartan Revolution* (Berkeley 1961).
F. Ollier, 'Le Philosophe Stoicien Sphairos et l'Oeuvre réformative des rois de Sparte Agis IV et Cleomène III', in *Revue des Études grecques*, 1936, 537 ff.

FOR BLOSSIUS:
T. S. Brown, 'Greek Influences on Tiberius Gracchus', in *Classical Journal*, 1941–42, 471 ff.
D. R. Dudley, 'Blossius of Cumae', *Journal of Roman Studies*, 1941, 94 ff.

FOR ARISTONICUS:
T. W. Africa, 'Aristonicus, Blossius and the City of the Sun', in *International Review of Social History*, 1961, 122–3.
F. Börner, *Untersuchungen über die Religion der Sklaven in Griechenland und Rom*, vol. III (Akademie der Wissenschaften und Literatur, Mainz, *Abhandlungen der geistes- und sozialwissenschaftlichen Klassen*, 1961, no. 4).
J. C. Dumont, 'A propos d'Aristonicos', in *Eirene*, 1966, 189 ff.
V. Vavřínek, *La révolte d'Aristonicos* (*Rozpravy Československé Akademie Věd*, 1957, no. 2).

FOR CLEOPATRA:
W. W. Tarn, 'Alexander Helios and the Golden Age', in *Journal of Roman Studies*, 1932, 135 ff.

FOR JUDAISM:
R. H. Charles, *Between the Old and New Testaments* (London 1914).

FOR CHRISTIANITY:
C. H. Dodd, *The Founder of Christianity* (London 1971).

V WITHDRAWAL

F. Allègre, *Étude sur la déesse grecque Tyché* (Lyon 1892).
J. Ferguson, *The Religions of the Roman Empire*, ch. 5 (London 1970).

ON ASTROLOGY:
A. Bouché-Leclerq, *L'astrologie grecque* (4 vols. Paris 1879–82).
F. Cumont, *Astrology and Religion among the Greeks and Romans* (London 1912).

ON EPICURUS:
E. Bignone, *L'Aristotele perduto e la formazione filosofica di Epicuro* (3 vols. Florence 1936).
N. W. De Witt, *Epicurus and his Philosophy* (Minneapolis 1957).
A. J. Festugière, *Epicure et ses Dieux* (Paris 1947).
R. D. Hicks, *Stoic and Epicurean* (London 1910).

ON THE CYNICS:
D. R. Dudley, *A History of Cynicism* (London 1938).

ON AUTARKY:
J. Ferguson, *Moral Values in the Ancient World*, ch. 8 (London 1958).

VI VARIETY

M. Bieber, *The Sculpture of the Hellenistic Age* (New York 1955).
G. Dickins, *Hellenistic Sculpture* (Oxford 1920).
A. W. Lawrence, *Later Greek Sculpture* (London 1927).
G. M. A. Richter, *Three Critical Periods in Greek Sculpture* (Oxford 1951).
T. B. L. Webster, *The Art of Greece: the Age of Hellenism* (New York 1966).
——, *Hellenistic Art* (London 1967).

VII LEARNING

FOR THE MUSEUM AND LIBRARY:
E. Badian, 'Ancient Alexandria', in *Studies in Greek and Roman History* (Oxford 1964).
E. A. Parsons, *The Alexandrian Library* (London 1952).

FOR THE SCHOLARSHIP:
R. Pfeiffer, *History of Classical Scholarship from the beginnings to the end of the Hellenistic Age* (Oxford 1968).

FOR PERGAMUM:
E. V. Hansen, *The Attalids of Pergamum* (New York 1947).

FOR THE DEVELOPMENTS IN SCIENCE:
T. W. Africa, *Science and the State in Greece and Rome* (New York 1968).
J. F. Dobson, 'Herophilus of Alexandria', in *Proceedings of the Royal Society of Medicine* (History of Medicine), 1925, 19–32.
O. Neugebauer, in *Proceedings of American Philosophical Society*, 1963, 530 ff.
——, *The Exact Sciences in Antiquity* (Copenhagen 1951).
P. Rousseau, *Histoire des Techniques* (Paris 1956).
G. Sarton, *A History of Science: Hellenistic Science and Culture in the last three centuries B.C.* (Cambridge, Mass. 1959).

FOR THE LITERATURE:
J. Ferguson, 'The Epigrams of Callimachus', in *Greece and Rome*, 1970, 64 ff.
A. S. F. Gow and D. Page, *Hellenistic Epigrams* (2 vols. Cambridge 1965–68).
R. Pfeiffer, *Callimachus* (2 vols. Oxford 1949–53).

VIII HUMANITY

FOR PHILANTHROPIA:
S. J. De Ruiter, 'De Vocis quae est *ΦΙΛΑΝΘΡΩΠΙΑ* significatione atque usu', in *Mnemosyne*, 1931, 271 ff.
J. Ferguson, *Moral Values in the Ancient World* (London 1958).
S. Lorenz, *De progressa actionis φιλανθρωπίας* (Leipzig 1914).

FOR PORTRAIT SCULPTURE:
A. Hekler, *Greek and Roman Portraits* (London 1912).
G. M. A. Richter, *The Portraits of the Greeks* (3 vols. London 1965).

FOR ARISTOTELIAN BIOGRAPHY:
F. Wehrli, *Die Schule des Aristoteles* (10 vols. Basle and Stuttgart 1944–59).

FOR APOLLONIUS:
J. F. Carspeeken, 'Apollonius Rhodius and the Homeric Epic', in *Yale Classical Studies*, 1952, 33 ff.

FOR THEOCRITUS:
A. S. F. Gow, *Theocritus* (2 vols. Cambridge 1950).

FOR HELLENISTIC LOVE POETRY:
An adequate treatment of this is much needed. Till this appears we have only the general studies of the period.

FOR 'THE SONG OF SONGS':
M. Rozelaar, in *Eshkolot*, pp. 33–48, (Jerusalem 1954). I owe the reference to M. Hadas, *Hellenistic Culture*, pp. 159–60 (New York 1959).

FOR THE ROMANCES:
A. Bonnard, *Greek Civilization: From Euripides to Alexandria* (London 1961).
B. Lavignani, *Studi sul romanzo greco* (Messina 1950).

FOR NEW COMEDY:
P. E. Legrand, *The New Greek Comedy* (Eng. transl. London 1917). Still as perceptive as anything, despite all the new discoveries. See also
T. B. L. Webster, *Studies in Menander* (Manchester 1950).
——, *Studies in Later Greek Comedy* (Manchester 1953).

FOR THEOPHRASTUS:
R. G. Ussher, *Theophrastus: The Characters* (London 1960).

IX DIVINITY

FOR RELIGION GENERALLY:
M. Gorce and R. Mortier, *Histoire générale des religions*, vol. II (Paris 1947).

FOR THE OLD GODS:
A. B. Cook, *Zeus: A Study in Ancient Religion* (3 vols. Cambridge 1914–40).
H. Jeanmaire, *Dionysos: Histoire du culte de Bacchus* (Paris 1951).
E. J. and L. Edelstein, *Asclepius* (2 vols. Baltimore 1945).

FOR SARAPIS:
T. S. Brady, 'The Reception of the Egyptian Cults by the Greeks 330–30 B.C.', in *University of Missouri Studies*, 1935.
P. M. Fraser, 'Two Studies of the Cult of Sarapis in the Hellenistic World', in *Opuscula Atheniensia*, 1960, 1–54.
E. Kiessling, 'La genèse du culte de Sarapis à Alexandrie', in *Chronique d'Egypte*, 1949, 317 ff.
P. Roussel, *Les Cultes égyptiennes à Délos* (Paris 1915–16).

FOR RULER-CULTS:

L. Cerfaux and J. Tondriau, *Un concurrent du christianisme: le culte des souverains dans la civilization gréco-romaine* (Paris 1957).

V. Ehrenberg, *The Greek State*, pp. 159–79 (2nd ed. London 1969).

E. Kornemann, 'Zur Geschichte der antiken Herrscherkulte', in *Klio*, 1901, 57 ff.

M. P. Nilsson, *Geschichte die griechische Religion*, vol. II (2nd ed. Munich 1960).

E. Skard, *Zwei religios-politische Begriff: Euergetes – Concordia* (Oslo 1932).

F. Taeger, *Charisma: Studien zur Geschichte des antiken Herrscherkulte*, vol. I (Stuttgart 1957).

——, 'Alexanders Gottkönigsgedanke und die Bewasstseinslage der Griechen und Makedonen', in *Numen*, Suppl. 4 (1959), 394 ff.

L. R. Taylor, *The Divinity of the Roman Emperor* (Middletown, Conn. 1931).

U. Wilcken, 'Zur Enstehung des hellenistischen Königskultes', in *Sitzungsberichte der preussischen Akademie der Wissenschaften, philosophische-historische Klasse*, Berlin, 1958.

FOR THE STOICS:

R. D. Hicks, *Stoic and Epicurean* (London 1910).

M. Pohlenz, *Die Stoa* (2 vols. Göttingen 1948–49).

FOR CHRYSIPPUS:

E. Bréhier, *Chrysippe et l'ancien stoïcisme* (2nd ed. Paris 1951).

J. B. Gould, *The Philosophy of Chrysippus* (Leiden 1970).

FOR POSEIDONIUS:

K. Reinhardt, *Poseidonios* (Heidelberg 1921).

——, 'Poseidonios', in Pauly-Wissowa, *Real-Encyclopädie der klassischen Altertumswissenschaft*, 22, 1953, 558–826.

X THE HERITAGE OF HELLENISM

A. Bonnard, *Greek Civilization* (Eng. transl. London 1957).

C. M. Bowra, *The Greek Experience* (London 1957).

S. H. Butcher, *Some Aspects of the Greek Genius* (London 1893).

——, *Harvard Lectures on the Originality of Greece* (London 1911).

G. L. Dickinson, *The Greek View of Life* (London 1896).

E. R. Dodds, *The Greeks and the Irrational* (Berkeley 1951).

Sir R. W. Livingstone, *The Greek Genius and its Meaning to Us* (Oxford 1912).

——, *Greek Ideals and Modern Life* (Oxford 1935).

—— (ed.), *The Legacy of Greece* (Oxford 1921).

A. Toynbee, *Hellenism* (London 1959).

CHRONOLOGICAL TABLE

BC	POLITICAL AND MILITARY EVENTS		EUROPE	ASIA
340			336–323 Alexander	
330				
320	323	Death of Alexander		
310	316	Cassander in Greece		313–280 Seleucus I
300	305–304	Siege of Rhodes		
	301	Battle of Ipsus		
290				
280	280–275	Pyrrhus in Italy and Sicily	276–239 Antigonus Gonatas	280–261 Antiochus I
270				263–241 Eumenes I (Pergamum)
260				261–247 Antiochus II
250				247–226 Seleucus II
240			239–229 Demetrius II	241–197 Attalus I (Pergamum)
230	c. 230	Attalus defeats Gauls	229–221 Antigonus Doson	226–223 Seleucus III
220	222	Battle of Sellasia	221–179 Philip V	223–187 Antiochus III
	218–203	Hannibal in Italy		
	217	Peace of Naupactus		
210	212	Sack of Syracuse		
200	202	Battle of Zama		
	197	Battle of Cynoscephalae		197–149 Eumenes II (Pergamum)
	196	Flamininus proclaims Greek freedom		

AFRICA	CULTURAL EVENTS
	341–270 Epicurus
	331 Foundation of Alexandria
323–283 Ptolemy I	322–264 Zeno at Stoa
	321 Menander's first play
	c. 310 Euhemerus
	c. 300 *Fortune of Antioch*
	c. 300 Euclid's *Elements*
	300 Foundation of Antioch
	c. 295? Foundation of Museum and Library
	293 Asclepius reaches Rome
	287 Archimedes b.
283–246 Ptolemy II	
	c. 280 Pharos of Alexandria
	275 Eratosthenes b.
	c. 270 Theocritus *fl.*
	Callimachus *fl.*
	Herondas *fl.*
	264–232 Cleanthes at Stoa
	c. 250 Aristarchus *fl.*
246–221 Ptolemy III	Apollonius of Rhodes *fl.*
	232–204 Chrysippus at Stoa
	c. 230–220 Gallic Monument at Pergamum
221–203 Ptolemy IV	
	212 Archimedes d.
203–181 Ptolemy V	

BC	POLITICAL AND MILITARY EVENTS	EUROPE	ASIA
190	189 Battle of Magnesia		
180		179–168 Perseus	175–168 Antiochus IV
170	168 Battle of Pydna		
160			159–133 Attalus III (Pergamum)
150	146 Sack of Carthage 146 Sack of Corinth	148 Macedonia a Roman province	
140	140–120 Slave risings 133 Tiberius Gracchus 133 Attalus III leaves Pergamum to Rome		
130			129 Asia a Roman province
	123 Gaius Gracchus		
120			
110			
100			
90	88 Sack of Delos		
80			
70			
60			64 Syria a Roman province
50			
40			
30	31 Battle of Actium		

AFRICA	CULTURAL EVENTS	
	_c._ 180	Altar of Zeus, Pergamum
	174	Foundation of Zeus Olympius, Athens
	161	Philosophers expelled from Rome
	_c._ 160	Library of Pergamum
	155	Philosophers in Rome
	_c._ 155	Polybius _fl._
	_c._ 150	Theatre at Priene
	_c._ 150	Stoa of Attalus, Athens
145–116 Ptolemy VII		
	_c._ 135–51	Poseidonius
	_c._ 100	Religious revival
	_c._ 100	_Venus de Milo_(?)
80–51 Ptolemy XI		
51–30 Cleopatra VII	_c._ 50	_Laocoön_(?)

LIST OF ILLUSTRATIONS

38 Epicurus; bust discovered on the Via Appia (copy after a 2nd-century BC original). Vatican Museum. Photo: Mansell

39 Zeno; bust copied from Greek original. Museo Nazionale, Rome, Collection Farnese. Photo: Anderson

40 Carneades of Cyrene; medallion from Holkham Hall, Norfolk. Photo: National Monuments Record

41 Silver dish showing a shepherd seated on a rock. Hermitage, Leningrad. Photo: courtesy Miss Gisela Richter

42 Gold diadem; found at Canosa. Museo Nazionale, Taranto. Photo: Soprintendenza alle Antichità, Taranto

43 Diogenes and Alexander; 1st century AD relief. Villa Albani, Rome. Photo: Mansell

44 Cynic, with wallet, flask and staff. Detail of fresco from the Farnesina garden. Museo Nazionale, Rome. Photo: Alinari

45 The *Fortune of Antioch*. Vatican Museum. Photo: Mansell

46 Colossal group representing *The Punishment of Dirce (Farnese Bull)*. Museo Nazionale, Naples. Photo: Anderson

47 Drunken old woman; Roman copy of an original 2nd-century BC sculpture. Staatliche Antikensammlungen, Munich

48 *Dying Gaul*; detail from the Gallic monument at Pergamum. Museo Nazionale, Ludovisi Collection. Photo: Leonard von Matt

49 Bronze statuette of a hunchback; Hellenistic, probably 2nd century BC. Museum für Kunst und Gewerbe, Hamburg

50 Terracotta of a nurse with a baby; from Boeotia, 330–200 BC. Courtesy Trustees of the British Museum, London

51 Dionysus and a satyr; gold *naiskos*, 250–200 BC. National Museum, Athens

52 Gold ear-ring from Tarentum, with wire and granulation patterns on the disc and pendant head of a woman; 4th century BC. Museo Nazionale, Taranto. Photo: Soprintendenza alle Antichità, Taranto

53 Theocritus' Pan pipe idyll; Aldine edition of 1495. British Museum, London. Photo: R.B. Fleming and Co.

54 Tombstone of Jason; marble relief, early 2nd century AD. Courtesy Trustees of the British Museum, London

55 A violet; illustration from *Materia Medica* of Dioscorides, early 6th century AD, annotated in Arabic. MS Med. gr. 1, fol. 148v. Österreichische Nationalbibliothek, Vienna

56 Illustration from Dionysius of Philadelphia's *Ornithiaca*. MS Med. gr. 1, fol. 483v. Österreichische Nationalbibliothek, Vienna

57 Navigational instrument found in the Dodecanese *c.* 1904; recovered from the Antikythera wreck, of the 1st century BC. National Museum, Athens

58 Archimedes' screw. Graeco-Roman terracotta, 1st century AD. Courtesy Trustees of the British Museum, London

59 The Tower of the Winds, Athens; detail showing Zephyrus (the west wind) and Lips (south-west wind); 1st century BC. Agora Excavations, American School of Classical Studies, Athens. Photo: Alison Frantz, Athens

60 Illustration from Hero's *Mechanica* (Arabic edition), showing tackle and pulley. Cod. ov. 51, Pg. 61. Department of Manuscripts, Bibliotheck der Rijksuniversiteit, Rapenburg

61 Dove mosaic; Roman copy of an original of the early 2nd century BC. Museo Capitolino, Rome. Photo: Alinari

62 Socrates; head found on the Via Appia, Rome. Vatican Museum. Photo: Alinari

63 Head of Arsinoe II; Hellenistic bronze. Museum of Fine Arts, Boston, Catherine Page Perkins Fund

64 Chrysippus; marble statue, *c.* 200 BC. Louvre, Paris. Photo: Giraudon

65 Demosthenes; Roman copy of a statue by Polyeuctus, erected 280 BC in the Athenian market-place. Ny Carlsberg Glyptothek, Copenhagen

66 Cleopatra VII; copper coin, 51–30 BC. British Museum, London. Photo: John Webb

67 Braggart soldier as a figure of Greek comedy; Hellenistic terracotta statuette from Asia Minor. Staatliche Museen, Berlin

68 Comic mask mosaic in the House of Menander, Mytilene. Courtesy *Antike Kirst*, Basel

69 Mosaic from the House of the Tragic Poet, Pompeii, 100 BC. Museo Nazionale, Naples. Photo: Leonard von Matt

70 Temple of Apollo at Didyma, begun *c.* 300 BC; the north-east face. Photo: Sonia Halliday

71 Alexander the Great wearing the horns of Ammon; obverse of a gold medallion from Aboukir. Staatliche Museen, Berlin

72 Colossal head of Zeus from Aegina, 1st century BC. Bildarchiv Foto Marburg

73 Colossal head of Apollo; bronze, 3rd century BC. Museo Provinciale, Salerno. Photo: Leonard von Matt

74 Head of young Dionysus in Parian marble; late Hellenistic. British Museum, London. Photo: Edwin Smith

75 Votive golden ear; from the Temple of Asclepius, Pergamum. Eigentum der Pergamon-Grabung

76 Asclepius and snake arriving on the Tiber island; Roman medallion of Antoninus Pius. British Museum, London. Photo: Ray Gardner

77 Poseidonius of Apamea; Roman bust, 70–60 BC. Museo Nazionale, Naples. Photo: Alinari

INDEX